TOUR DE FRANCE/TOUR DE FORCE

A VISUAL HISTORY OF THE WORLD'S GREATEST BICYCLE RACE   UPDATED AND REVISED

BY JAMES STARTT   INTRODUCTION BY GREG LEMOND   PREFACE BY SAMUEL ABT

CHRONICLE BOOKS

SAN FRANCISCO

TO MY PARENTS, JIM AND CATHY, AND MY WIFE, REBEKAH

A hardcover edition of this book was originally published in 2000 by Chronicle Books LLC.
Text copyright © 2000, 2003 by James Startt.

Page 158 constitutes a continuation of the copyright page.

Library of Congress Cataloging-in-Publication Data available:
Startt, James, 1962–
Tour de France, Tour de Force : a visual history of the world's greatest bicycle race / by James Startt.
p. cm.
Includes bibliographical references.
ISBN: 0-8118-3906-0
1. Tour de France (bicycle race) — History. 2. Tour de France (bicycle race) Pictorial works. I. Title.
GV1049.2.T68S73 2000
796.6'2'0944—dc21   99-23740
                          CIP
Manufactured in China.
Design: C2

Distributed in Canada by Raincoast Books
9050 Shaughnessy Street
Vancouver, British Columbia V6P 6E5

10 9 8 7 6 5 4 3 2

Chronicle Books LLC
85 Second Street
San Francisco, CA 94105

www.chroniclebooks.com

COVERS:

Front Cover: America's Lance Armstrong rides his way towards his first Tour victory in 1999.

Back Cover: Italy's Gino Bartali rolls towards his first Tour victory in 1938.

PREVIOUS PAGES:

page 1 A dapper Petit-Breton stands for a portrait session with his bicycle.

page 2 In his familiar position at the front, Petit-Breton leads the pack through the crowd-filled village during the 1908 race.

page 3 René Van-Meenen, just one of the faceless water bottle carriers of the Tour, works his way back toward the pack with a fresh supply of drinks for his teammates. Hardly more than a disposable pawn in the big picture, he would never finish the 1963 Tour.

page 4 Frenchman Richard Virenque, one of the sport's most charismatic and controversial figures, plunges off the start ramp into the 1995 Tour de France.

page 5 Eddy Merckx chases his young rival, Bernard Thévenet, on the Izoard Pass during the 1975 race.

page 6 First come, first served pretty well sums up the mood at a 1927 Tour de France feed zone.

page 7 Factory workers in Brittany take a break to watch the 1997 Tour pass.

page 8 Switzerland's Alex Zülle gets mechanical help after crashing in the 1993 Tour. Unfortunately for Zülle, this would not be the last untimely crash of his career.

BACK PAGES:

page 159 Lance Armstrong leads his U.S. Postal Service team in the team time trial during the 2002 race.

page 160 Although he would eventually lose his green jersey to Australia's Robbie McEwen (left), Germany's Erik Zabel (center) was only too happy to win this stage into Alencon during the 2002 Tour.

TABLE OF CONTENTS

WAR STORIES FROM A WINNER:

INTRODUCTION BY GREG LEMOND

I returned to the Tour de France in 1998 as a spectator. That was the first time I'd been to the race since I had to drop out in 1994. And frankly, the thought of going back was a bit painful. Why, you may be wondering, would it be painful for the three-time winner of the world's greatest bike race to return? Well, I guess it's the memories. There are just too many to face. The highs—and there were plenty—don't get much higher. But the lows, oh, they don't get much lower. At the Tour, there is simply no middle ground. On the one hand, winning it is the ultimate achievement. It's like winning the Super Bowl every day for three weeks, or like winning a three-week-long New York City Marathon. Pretty hard to believe? You can say that again.

On the other hand, you also know that you'll never match such an experience again. Perhaps only a race like the Tour can do that to you. It's funny, but long after my career was over, I still had dreams about it. Heck, just the other night I woke up dreaming I was racing in the Tour again, hearing the crowds go crazy and pushing up some mountain.

So what makes the Tour what it is? What is its magic? For one thing, its history sparks the imagination. Just like the Olympics, the Tour creates dreams and inspires us. And because of those dreams, it brings out the best in people.

When I was a kid there was a bike race outside my house in Nevada. Already I had vaguely heard about this thing called the Tour de France. Then when I started to ride, I met Roland Della Santa, a local frame builder. I'd go to his house and look through all those old *Miroir du Cyclisme* magazines and all those photographs. The drama simply spoke for itself. And as soon as I started racing, the Tour became my goal, as it does for just about any kid starting out. But when I was growing up in the States in the 1970s, nobody knew anything about the Tour de France. Little matter that it was the world's biggest annual sporting event. I just

couldn't believe it. For me that only added to its mystique, because here was this huge worldwide event every year that was completely removed from everything that was important to Americans at the time.

By the time I was seventeen I'd raced in Europe. That's also about the same time I realized that Europeans actually weren't from outer space. They could win or lose just like anybody else. Already back then I was winning a lot. So, logically, or so it seemed to me at the time, my goal became winning the Tour. I remember writing my career goals down on a legal pad. The last one was to win the Tour by the time I was twenty-five.

It's crazy, but I did it, although the path to Tour victory wasn't as clear as it sounds. Frankly, there were times when those goals were the only thing that kept me going. In those first years when I was breaking into European professional life, I

12

sure needed them. They helped me to put up with the bad salaries, the weather in France in February—you name it.

One thing that most people fail to realize is what it takes to get there, to the top of the sport. Most of cycling is not the Tour de France. It's not glamorous. And a lot of it is just plain hard, ugly, and miserable. The Tour is not just a race you enter. It's a whole career. You don't just say, "I'm going to ride the Tour this year." And in those first years, if I hadn't had the Tour in my head, I would probably just have packed it in. But the Tour is one of those things that goes beyond frustration, fear, and fatigue.

Before I ever won it, I had to learn a lot about life, all of which is wrapped up in that little microcosm of cycling. Professional cycling is a cutthroat world: you're only as good as your last race. Until I raced professionally for a while, I didn't believe that people had ulterior motives. Naive? I sure was. But along the way I learned about a lot of things, and I learned them on the bike. I had to learn to deal with the problems within my own team, not to mention problems with my one-time idol and mentor, Bernard Hinault.

But I always knew that things would sort themselves out come Tour time. For a cyclist, you see, the Tour is the ultimate proving ground. Luck is minimized, and the strongest always win.

I'll never forget that first victory in 1986. I was totally drained from my battle with Hinault. He had promised to work for me after my support for him in 1985. But then when he saw that he had a chance to win a historic sixth Tour, well, no Frenchman could pass up such a chance. But there was no way I was going to lose the race that year. And to have finally won, and to have beaten a legend like Hinault, wow, that's a satisfaction I'll never know again. You see, there is a hierarchy in bike racing. It is understood by the riders. And everybody knew what it took to beat a guy like Hinault in his race, on his turf.

But in some ways I don't think I really realized what it meant until I tried to come back after my hunting accident. I guess the only way to appreciate some things is after suffering a little setback.

Getting shot was more than a "little setback," and it definitely put the Tour in a new perspective. For most of the time between 1987 and 1989, I felt I'd fallen far from my previous level. Even in the 1989 Tour of Italy, I suffered so much that I was looking at the other guys in awe. And that was only weeks from the 1989 Tour de France.

I entered that year's Tour with a lot of question marks. It was my first Tour in three years. Early on I hoped simply to come out in the top twenty. But then I won that first time trial and put on my yellow jersey again and that changed everything. I told my wife, Cathy, "This is where I belong." I didn't tell the press, but with that jersey on my shoulders, I knew nobody was going to beat me. I would have to die first. That is how much the Tour can motivate.

When I went back to the Paris hotel after finally winning, I felt like I was in a fairy tale. It was just incredible to have won the Tour again. But I remember telling Cathy, "I'm just not a second-place rider. Not in the Tour at least." And when I returned a year later for the 1990 Tour, there was no doubt for me. I was going to repeat.

You see, motivation really is a huge factor. Sometimes when I look back, I don't know how I won those last two Tours. To be competitive you have to be in top physical form but also be fresh. That is a very fine line to walk. Every year I raced, preparing was pure trial and error. Getting back to my old level after that hunting accident was very difficult, and I did plenty of things wrong. I knew how to prepare when I was fit, but not when I was unfit. Most of that time I was chasing after good form. And frankly, I was only fresh a couple of times after my accident. But fortunately those times most often happened in July.

I went into the 1991 Tour with that same mind-set, that same confidence. But it didn't work the way I'd planned. I struggled on the first day in the mountains, and that totally deflated me. I can still remember the moment when I was getting dropped on the Tourmalet. I was crushed—just shattered. I probably should have quit, but I just couldn't imagine doing it. When you think you're unbeatable, the first defeat is just devastating. You

think you can come back. You tell yourself as much. But you're just buying time. That first defeat changes you forever. And it's then, when things aren't going right, that you really realize just how hard winning the Tour is. That's why Miguel Indurain retired after his first defeat in 1996.

When I look back, more than any other race, I am grateful to have been able to win the Tour de France. The Tour is three weeks of constant drama. The sport is so competitive that there is no room for mistakes. The drama is so high, it is like an ongoing soap opera. Wheelings and dealings are constant. Pack diplomacy is essential. To win the Tour you also have to know how to lose. Nobody can win every day, every stage. You've got to pick and choose, play your cards right. There are plenty of unspoken ethics. When you're wearing the yellow jersey, for instance, you don't kill somebody's chances for a stage win when it's not important to the overall lead. If you do, you will make some enemies fast. And then there's the whole psychological aspect of being on top every day. It's constant paranoia; every day is a new test.

But France is a magical place for such a race, and everything comes together for the Tour. They close the country down for you. The roads take on their own identity. There is a romance to them, and they belong to the Tour. You couldn't have this race in any other country.

Some days start out slow and relaxed, but you know that by the end of the day you're going to be racing at incredible speeds, taking incredible risks. The adrenaline of the *peloton* infects you. Sometimes we riders can't even believe how fast we go. I remember one day in 1992. We had just finished a grueling stage. On paper it was a nothing stage. But we rode so hard the entire day. I don't know who was driving the pace, but we maintained nearly fifty kph (thirty mph), and that's including two stops for trains. Most of us were just hanging on for dear life, and by the end we were just wasted. All I remember afterward was looking over at Charly Mottet, who was about as shell-shocked as I was. We just stared at each other and shook our heads. One word sufficed. "*Incroyable*," he said. Yes, incredible.

A BUNCH OF GUYS PEDALING IN THEIR UNDERWEAR:

PREFACE BY SAMUEL ABT

For the first five years after I moved to Paris from New York in 1971, the only sports that still mattered to me were the ones I grew up playing and watching. Through blizzards of static I listened on a short-wave radio to the Armed Forces Network in Germany (France had expelled all American soldiers years before) as it broadcast baseball and football games from home. Television showed only soccer or rugby matches and the infrequent bicycle race—all of them incomprehensible sports, especially bicycle racing, which, in a phrase I liked to repeat then, was merely a bunch of guys pedaling in their underwear.

The person I liked to repeat that phrase to was the woman with whom I was living in Paris, an American also and one with many interests and even passions. They included, in no particular order, the cello, physics, anything Spanish, badminton, acoustics, me, and bicycle racing. I was indifferent to most of these, with bicycle racing near the top of the list. When, for example, she invited me in 1974 to join her in watching the finish of the Tour de France at the Stade Municipal de Vincennes in the east of Paris, I ostentatiously chose instead to spend the day with a friend in a forest west of Paris, hunting for mushrooms.

What made it ostentatious was that I had never looked for mushrooms before, as she well knew, and never did again. Although my friend and I did find quite a few of the big, meaty kind that the French call cèpes and had them for dinner that night in a tasty omelet, it was the worst trade-off since Esau gave away his birthright for a mess of gruel; I realized, years later, that I had blown my chance to see not only the last finish of the Tour in the Vincennes velodrome—after that the race ended on the Champs-Elysées—but also the last Tour won by Eddy Merckx.

I caught up with Merckx, or the shell he had become, in 1977. By then, in a feverish swirl of office politics, I had moved from being news editor of the *International Herald Tribune* to sports editor, a less demanding job and one out of the line of fire. My "roommate" and I had married by then and had a son, and I decided, obliging fellow that I was, to show my wife a good time by assigning myself to cover a bicycle race and bringing her along. No point in starting at the bottom or even the middle: The first race I saw was the prologue to the sixty-fourth Tour de France, on June 30, 1977, in the town of Fleurance in the southwest, my favorite part of France for eating, drinking, and sightseeing. Off the family went, all expenses paid. So what if I had to justify the trip by writing about a bicycle race? That couldn't be too difficult—it was, after all, just a bunch of guys pedaling in their underwear.

As I write this, I am looking at the clipping of my first article about the sport, in which I reported that Didi Thurau, a twenty-two-year-old German, won the prologue (which I called "a trial sprint," whatever that meant) over Gerrie Knetemann, twenty-six, a Dutchman, with Merckx, thirty-three (whom I described, accurately, as both a veteran and the people's choice), no factor. A possibly indifferent world learned from me that Knetemann's performance was no surprise since he was "a sprint specialist" and had no long-range future in the Tour, but that Thurau's was a stunner and promised much since he was "considered to be of longer-lasting quality." Not that I was the one doing the considering. That was the counsel of Emile Besson, the correspondent of *l'Humanite Dimanche*, the French Communist newspaper, next to whom, by chance, I was sitting in the covered market that served as a pressroom for the thirty or forty—now three or four hundred—reporters

with the Tour. A kindly man, now retired but still to be seen sometimes at Tour and team presentations, Besson took the time to instruct me that Thurau had already won the Tour of Andalusia in Spain that year and had finished second, to Knetemann, in the Grand Prix of Frankfurt. Those details stood out in my article, testimony to my intimate knowledge of the sport. When Thurau continued to hold the yellow jersey for the next two weeks, my reputation was made to editors of both the *Herald Tribune* and the *New York Times*, which have published my work ever since. (My reputation was slightly unmade two weeks later after the climb to Chamonix, when Thurau lost the jersey to Bernard Thévenet, the eventual winner of that Tour, and I wrote that "this territory seems tailored for Lucien van Impe, last year's winner"; but nobody should blame Besson for that bit of expertise. By then I considered myself so knowledgeable that I needed nobody's counsel. After all, I had been following the sport for a full two weeks.)

By then, also and of course, I was hooked. The color, the speed, the glorious scenery, the companionship, the pageantry, the sheer athletic skill of the riders, their availability and willingness to talk—all thrilled me then and still do, after more than twenty years of watching and writing about the sport.

My second piece about the Tour was a portrait of Merckx: "When he mounted the starting ramp, the crowd pressed in, the cheers grew louder, the cameramen swarmed around and fathers lifted their small children for a look at Merckx in his final Tour de France." One of those fathers was me, and one of those small children was my son, John, then not quite nine months old. His mother lifted him for a look at Merckx too. People remember that they saw Eddy Merckx in the Tour, even if only once. Bike racing is a sport that, for a lucky few, you have to see only once to love.

ONE OF THE RARE ACTION IMAGES OF THE INAUGURAL TOUR DE FRANCE. OBVIOUSLY
THE CHOICE OF APPROPRIATE RACING GEAR WAS LEFT LARGELY UP TO THE BIKERS.
EVENTUAL WINNER MAURICE GARIN IS IN THE WHITE PULLOVER.

1903–1914: THE PIONEER YEARS

The whole world, it seemed, was booming in the 1890s. For the French it was known as the *belle époque*. The Industrial Revolution was in full swing, and nearly everyone reportedly came under its spell.

For many, the bicycle was a symbol of this new age: it was affordable and gave mobility to the masses. And although sports stardom was only a fledgling concept, there were plenty of heroes. Track racing held center stage, but with the birth of a new century, bicycle road racing began to take over.

In keeping with the spirit of the age, cycling organizers in France had grandiose visions. Cyclists crossed vast parts of the country racing in mythic events such as Bordeaux-Paris or Paris-Brest-Paris, the latter of which was organized by French journalist Pierre Giffard. With an imagination to fit his ego, Giffard announced, "I want a race that will go to the end of the earth"—and for the French at that time, the coastal town of Brest pretty much fit the bill. "P-B-P" was an instant success, drawing hordes of enthusiasts. And as a result, *Le Petit Journal*, Giffard's paper, boasted a huge sales growth.

The competing sports daily *L'Auto-Vélo*—known later as *L'Auto*—was not about to be one-upped or outpedaled. Their response was to organize an even larger event: the Tour de France Cycliste.

Two of the newspaper's employees, Géo Lefèvre and Henri Desgrange, masterminded the Herculean competition. Lefèvre envisioned "something like a six-day [track] race, but on roads around France." Although initially skeptical, Desgrange warmed to the idea, eventually taking it under his wing. It proved to be the best move of his life.

Today he is credited with being the father of the Tour de France: Lefèvre may have come up with the idea, but Desgrange made it happen. The *maillot jaune*, or leader's yellow jersey, bore the initials *H. D.* from 1919, when it became part of the race, until 1983.

1903: HISTORIC RISK AND HISTORIC SUCCESS Uncertainty clouded the first Tour race. Sponsors, after all, were assuming great financial risks, and the cyclists were essentially riding into the unknown.

True to the six-day concept of track racing, the first Tour was only six stages long, but each stage was a grueling ultramarathon: Paris-Lyon, Lyon-Marseilles, Marseilles-Toulouse, Toulouse-Bordeaux, Bordeaux-Nantes, and Nantes-Paris. Stages, which averaged four hundred kilometers in length, often ran through the night. By the time the race returned to Paris, those who finished would feel an additional 2,428 kilometers in their legs.

To cajole riders into an event that many considered insane—and to ensure the competition's survival—race directors baited the field with a twenty-thousand-franc prize purse. Still, on May 6, just weeks before the start of the race, the list of participants barely hovered around twenty. In a last-ditch effort to entice newcomers, the newspaper cut the entry fee in half, lowering it to ten francs. And after *L'Auto* decided to pay the top fifty riders in each stage five francs to help with expenses, organizers were able to lure a solid sixty riders to the start line. Finishing the first Tour de France, however, would certainly cost a lot more than money.

Although a sports feat of this magnitude had never taken place, two prerace favorites emerged: Frenchmen Hippolyte Aucouturier and Maurice Garin. Few foreign riders made the top-contender list, but then the first Tour de France was primarily a "Tour de French." Although there were some foreign riders in the mix—primarily Belgians—the race was not yet the international rendez-vous it is today.

Aucouturier, having just snagged Paris-Roubaix and Bordeaux-Paris, was the odds-on favorite. Garin's chances were harder to estimate. After all, he had bolstered his reputation with more eclectic races such as the "Twenty-Four Hours of the Liberal Arts," or the "Eight Hundred Kilometers of Paris"—not exactly established references in the sport. But he had also won the respected Paris-Roubaix and just months before the Tour, he added Paris-Brest-Paris to his collection of victories.

Garin led after the first stage, but Aucouturier took the next two. By the time the peloton reached Toulouse, Aucouturier had an easy lead. Physically, however, this Tour stuff was taking its toll, and stomach troubles finally got the best of him. Specialists claimed that he drank too much water! Forced to drop out, Aucouturier went down as the first significant casualty of the Tour. He would not be the last.

As Aucouturier faded, Garin blazed to victory—he still holds the record for the largest winning margin: two hours and forty-nine minutes.

1904: A TUMULTUOUS TURNAROUND *Fair play*, more than one Frenchman has said, is a British term used by the British when the British win. Well, in the second edition of the young French race, there weren't any Brits, or for that matter, much in the way of fair play.

On July 2, 1904, the race began without a hitch, following the same route as the year before. "Don't fix it if it ain't broke," the race organizers seemed to be saying. But if the first Tour went smoothly enough, the second nearly self-destructed after it was infected with cheating and outright sabotage.

Maurice Garin, the defending champion and overwhelming favorite, led the team La Française with his brother César and 1903 runner-up Lucien Pothier. Garin was the designated leader, with Pothier promising to pick up the relay in the event of any setbacks. But they faced stiff competition from another remarkable squad, Peugeot, which was led by the ever-hungry Aucouturier.

Late into the first stage, Garin and Pothier broke away from the pack. But as they headed into the Lyon suburbs, they were cut off by a car full of fans of a rival competitor. For six kilometers, the cyclists battled with the driver, who tried to run them into a ditch. Apparently, in the eyes of these fans, all was fair in love and sport.

Such run-ins with zealous, sometimes vengeful, fans only continued. During stage two, Frenchman

TOUR DE FRANCE FINISHERS FROM THE 1903 RACE PREPARE TO TAKE A FINAL VICTORY LAP AROUND THE PARC DES PRINCES VÉLODROME IN PARIS. SINCE THE TOUR'S INCEPTION, TRADITION HAS HELD THAT EVERY TOUR FINISHER MUST TAKE AN HONORARY LAP. WINNER MAURICE GARIN IS THE SECOND RIDER FROM THE LEFT.

André Faure attacked shortly after 3:00 A.M. on the hills surrounding the industrial city of Saint-Étienne, his home region. He was followed by Pothier, and the two whizzed over the crest of a hill. But when the rest of the pack arrived—surprise! They couldn't pass. Instead, they faced a mob of Faure's fans, who had formed a human blockade. The fans even began attacking Garin and throwing rocks. Organizers eventually had to break out pistols and fire into the air to disperse the crowd.

Later, spectators revolted when a little-known rider from southern France, Payan d'Alès, was disqualified for repeated drafting violations. Angry fans warned that the Tour would never make it through Nîmes, which was close to d'Alès's hometown. They scattered nails and broken glass on the road as the Tour approached the city's gates, and when it reached the

center of Nîmes, they attacked the competitors. Again, only gunshots could stop the mob.

The race finally managed to stagger back to Paris, but reports of cheating and violence came pouring in to officials. Although it seemed that everyone took part—the fans, sponsors, and cyclists—in the eyes of the officials, the worst violators were the race's top riders. Four months after the race, the Vélocipèdique de France, the national cycling federation, penalized twenty-nine riders and disqualified the top four finishers: the Garin brothers, Pothier, and Aucouturier. Pothier suffered an even worse fate: he was banned from racing for life.

By default, the officials named a new winner, twenty-year-old Henri Cornet of France. And nearly a century later, he is still the youngest winner in

Tour history. Fifth place for a twenty-year-old first timer is considered respectable by any standard. But after being declared winner by default, Cornet was awarded the nickname "Rigolo," or "the Phony." And although he tried to erase his moniker with a legitimate victory, he never succeeded.

After the fiasco of the 1904 race, Desgrange initially declared the race over. "Killed by success," he wrote. In the end, however, the Tour would continue, but unfortunately so would the cheating. In 1907 three riders were disqualified for actually taking a train to cut the stage short. But such events no longer dominated the headlines, as the racing itself increasingly captured the public's imagination.

RIDERS IN ECHELON FORMATION RACE TOWARD LUNEVILLE IN EASTERN FRANCE DURING THE 1909 RACE .

MAURICE GARIN: NOT BAD FOR A CHIMNEY SWEEP

GARIN POSES FOR A PORTRAIT AFTER WINNING THE FIRST TOUR WITH HIS MASSEUR DRESSED IN BUTCHERS BIB ON THE RIGHT AND GARIN'S SON ON THE LEFT.

THE CELEBRATED COUNT ZEPPELIN, INTRIGUED BY THIS SPECTACLE CALLED THE TOUR DE FRANCE, VISITS THE 1907 RACE AT THE FINISH IN METZ. HERE HE GREETS THE 1905 WINNER LOUIS TROUSSELIER.

The first Tour de France needed a winner with a vision as vast as the race itself; someone who understood the magnitude of the challenge and confronted it with similar courage. Maurice Garin pretty much fit the bill.

In fact, race director Henri Desgrange couldn't have hoped for a more appropriate winner that first year. Garin epitomized the spirit of the turn of the century: he was the picture of confidence, and what more could race organizers hope for than a cycling champion with a handlebar mustache?

Like Desgrange, Garin was known for his toughness, something he picked up from his meager beginnings as a chimney sweep. But once this Italian immigrant discovered cycling, he gladly traded chimney soot for athletic sweat. At the end of the nineteenth century, the "Little Chimney Sweep," as he was affectionately called, established himself as a major champion. He twice won the legendary Paris-Roubaix classic, and after he went on to win ultralong races like Paris-Brest-Paris and Bordeaux-Paris, he was recognized as one of the top dogs of his day.

At the start of the first Tour de France, Garin was already thirty-two—an age when many cyclists are tempted to retire. Garin, however, was tempted by the new challenge. Before the 1903 start he boasted: "Oh, I know that it [the Tour] is going to be hard, but that doesn't matter. That's what I want. It has to be hard. The sun will be hot. So much the better. The short rests between the stages will make the first hundred kilometers of each stage terrible. So much the better." Words like these couldn't have made Henri Desgrange happier.

Garin fulfilled the expectations of everyone, including Desgrange. He won three of the six stages of the inaugural Tour and easily took the overall prize.

In 1904 Garin again won the first stage from Paris to Lyon, and he rolled easily to his second Tour victory. After the 1904 Tour finished, however, numerous accounts of foul play surfaced. Illegal teamwork and out-and-out sabotage were the most often cited infractions. For most, survival was based on the rules of the road, not on the rule books. Just about everyone, it seems, was implicated, but Garin was one of the riders who suffered most. He, along with the rest of the top four finishers, was disqualified. Needless to say, his image slipped in Desgrange's eyes.

Garin would never ride the Tour again, and, unlike champions nearly a century later, he didn't retire rich and famous. In keeping with his blue-collar background, he invested in a filling station in northern France and worked the pumps until he died at the age of eighty-five.

TOUR DE FRANCE RIDERS START THE 1906 RACE.

A HAGGARD EMILE GEORGET (RIGHT), ONE OF THE TOP
PRE–WORLD WAR I FAVORITES, PAUSES FOR A BREATHER
DURING THE 1906 TOUR WITH MAURICE GARIN (LEFT),
WHO WAS SIMPLY A SPECTATOR THAT YEAR.

A POSTCARD PORTRAIT OF PETIT-BRETON IN 1909.

1907–1908: PETIT-BRETON, A TOUR-STYLED HERO

ALTHOUGH PETIT-BRETON IS REMEMBERED AS THE FIRST TWO-TIME WINNER OF THE TOUR, HE WAS ALSO A HIGHLY RESPECTED TRACK RIDER.

With his upset Victory in the 1907 race, everyone agreed—the Tour de France had found a true original in Petit-Breton. Fittingly, Petit-Breton's true identity is never easy to pinpoint. For starters, he had three names. Born Lucien Mazan, he acquired the nickname "the Argentinean" after spending several years racing his bike in Buenos Aires. And before that, he had invented the name Breton for himself when he signed up for his first bike race. That was the only way he could keep his father, an unsuccessful wanna-be politician, from seeing his name in the result columns of the paper's sports section. Bike racing, according to papa Mazan, was nothing short of "dishonor to the family name." But it was this fictional name that stuck, and Mazan was affectionately known as Petit-Breton throughout his career.

On the bike, Petit-Breton was equally hard to identify. Was he a sprinter or a pursuit specialist? One thing was certain—he was a phenomenon. He broke the world hour record in 1905 and rode in the greatest six-day track races. Although he was often outclassed by the gods of the boards like

Major Taylor, he was a constant crowd pleaser. "Once I get on the track I can't control my patience," he once said.

But Petit-Breton was never able to rein in his emotions; he rode with his heart. Adrenaline was the key to his success. One of his most memorable emotionally inspired performances came in 1904 when he was pitted against Léon "the Brutal" Georget in a twenty-four-hour pursuit race. After sprinting out to an early advantage, Petit-Breton nearly fainted from exhaustion and was forced to take a break. Shaking his head and icing his feet, he insisted that he was throwing in the towel. But when Georget made a pit stop of his own, Petit-Breton became rejuvenated. Back on his bike, he quickly made up the forty-three-minute deficit and the next day was declared the winner.

Only in the Tour de France, however, did his true identity surface. Here he was both a crowd pleaser and a champion, and his strong character made him the perfect Tour hero.

In 1907 he surprised the prerace favorites when he won the race as a *poinçonnée* (a special independent category). After laying low during the first half of the race, he attacked early on the Toulouse-Bayonne stage. Although two hundred kilometers still separated him from the finish, he held on to win the stage and took control of the race.

The next year he became the first double winner and he nearly became the first triple winner in 1913. Only a crash in the penultimate stage prevented him from winning the race for a third time. Locked in a tight battle with Belgian Philippe Thys throughout much of the race, Petit-Breton saw his chances evaporate midway through the fateful stage when he fell and landed hard on his knee. Heartbroken, he abandoned the race. What he did not know, however, was that just up the road, Thys had also crashed and had been completely knocked out. If he had managed to continue, he likely would have dropped the delirious Thys. But Petit-Breton was unaware of his competitor's misfortune. He had already thrown in the towel. And this time it was for good.

PETIT-BRETON
ACKNOWLEDGES A
FAN BEFORE TAKING
A VICTORY LAP
AFTER WINNING HIS
FIRST TOUR IN 1907.

AFTER BREAKING HIS CHAIN IN THE LAST KILOMETER, LUXEMBOURG'S FABER RUNS HIS BIKE ACROSS THE FINISH LINE DURING THE 1909 TOUR. BUT FABER HAS PLENTY OF TIME—AFTER THE 309-KILOMETER STAGE FROM BELFORT TO LYON, HIS NEAREST COMPETITOR IS OVER TEN MINUTES DOWN.

FABER POSES AFTER WINNING THE 1909 TOUR.

THE BEEFY FRANÇOIS FABER FLATTENED HIS OPPONENTS WITH HIS POWER. BUT WHEN THE TOUR ENTERED THE MOUNTAINS IN 1910, FABER WAS HUMBLED. WITH HIS OXLIKE BUILD HE HAD LITTLE CHANCE OF RIVALING THE REAL CLIMBERS.

1910: AIN'T NO MOUNTAIN HIGH ENOUGH . . . SORT OF

1910 TOUR WINNER OCTAVE LAPIZE SMILES AT THE EQUALLY STRANDED PHOTOGRAPHER AS HE WALKS HIS BIKE THROUGH AN ISOLATED MOUNTAIN PASS IN THE PYRENEES.

CASHING IN ON TOUR DE FRANCE FAME, THIS POSTER ADVERTISES LAPIZE BICYCLES, NAMED AFTER THE 1910 WINNER.

At first Tour director Henri Desgrange appeared dumbfounded when he was presented with the idea of taking the Tour into the high mountains of the Pyrenees. "Are you crazy?" was his response. After all, such obscure mountain roads were little more than cow paths in 1910. According to legend, even bears could be seen along the route.

But wasn't this reaction similar to the one he had had to the initial idea of a Tour de France Cycliste? In both cases he eventually embraced the challenge and transformed it into a huge success.

The three previous races had followed virtually the same circuit. After the original introduction of the Ballon d'Alsace climb in 1905, the mountains offered a sure way to spice things up a bit. So in 1910 the riders trudged up some of the toughest climbs the Pyrenees had to offer. During two excruciating days, the cyclists pumped, grunted, and groaned over the soon-to-be-legendary climbs like the Aspin, Peyresourde, Tourmalet, and Aubisque. Many simply walked.

"*Assassins!*" That was Octave Lapize's reaction as he made his way past the race directors mid-

way up the Col d'Aubisque. But then Lapize really couldn't have had too many problems with the new race route—he ended up winning the 1910 race.

One thing was clear. The introduction of the high mountains forever changed the face of the Tour and its champions. Immense power-based riders, like 1909 winner François Faber, would no longer be able to dominate. Versatility now became the crucial prerequisite.

And despite the initial displeasure of some riders, the mountains offered the Tour its most dramatic stage.

TOUR DE FRANCE CYCLISTE 1910

Arrivée du premier peloton au Parc des Princes, 1er Ernest Azzini - 2e Ernest Paul - 3e Menager

A POSTCARD FROM THE FINAL STAGE INTO PARIS SHOWS ERNEST AZZINI (CENTER) EDGING OUT
ERNEST PAUL (LEFT) AND CONSTANT MENAGER (RIGHT) FOR VICTORY IN THE PARC DES PRINCES.

EMILE GEORGET (LEFT) AND PETIT-BRETON (RIGHT) SMILE AFTER SIGNING IN AT THE STAGE FINISH IN NICE. NOTICE PETIT-BRETON'S YELLOW JERSEY. NO, HE IS NOT WEARING IT BECAUSE HE IS THE RACE LEADER. CYCLISTS WERE ALREADY KNOWN FOR THEIR COLORFUL CLOTHING, BUT THE YELLOW JERSEY WOULD NOT BECOME THE OFFICIAL LEADER'S JERSEY FOR NEARLY ANOTHER DECADE.

WITH HIS MIDSIZED BUILD, BELGIUM'S PHILIPPE THYS WAS THE PERFECT TOUR RIDER.

1913–1920: THYS'S TRIPLE

A HAPPY PHILIPPE THYS AT THE PARIS FINISH IN 1913 WITH THE FIRST OF HIS THREE WINNER'S BOUQUETS.

Philippe Thys is remembered as one of the first true Tour de France specialists. He did ride other races, but he rarely won them. The Tour, however, became his fetish race. For the Belgian it was a worthwhile fixation, and he led the first wave of Belgian riders that dominated every Tour from 1912 to 1922 (countryman Odile DeFraye won the 1912 event). During those years of Belgian domination, Thys became the first three-time winner in the history of the Tour, a feat that went untouched until Louison Bobet pulled off the triple in the 1950s.

For Thys the race was nothing short of Herculean in its challenge. Inherently he understood that winning it would require equally Herculean prepa-

ration. And with a hard-work ethic that would have humbled Henry Ford, he went about preparing for the world's biggest bike race. In his hometown of Brussels, he earned the reputation of a training monster. Reportedly, he would often awake before dawn and set out on marathon training rides in the dark. Then, upon his return, he would often complement the ride with a long hike.

Often, Thys was not the most brilliant rider in the Tour. Unlike his contemporaries, such as the charismatic and powerful François Faber, Thys was not concerned with stage wins. Overall victory counted most, and to achieve it he relied on steadfast consistency. From his first participation, he

was always well placed, and with each Tour Thys evolved more into a top contender.

Twice (in 1913 and 1914) on the same stage from Longwy to Dunkerque, he crashed and broke his fork, thus placing his victory in jeopardy. On both occasions, however, Thys calculated his advance perfectly and managed to repair his bike with enough time left to hold onto the lead.

As a member of the mighty Peugeot team, Thys won his first two Tours in 1913 and 1914; and he won again in 1920. World War I, however, proved to be his one insurmountable adversary. If it were not for the forced four-year hiatus, Thys's victory count would likely have surpassed three.

THE PACK HUSTLES THROUGH A FEED ZONE DURING THE 1912 TOUR.

FEW CONSIDERED BELGIUM'S FIRMIN LAMBOT A POTENTIAL WINNER, BUT AFTER WORLD WAR I, THE PICKINGS AMONG THE TOP CYCLISTS WERE SLIM, AND LAMBOT PROVED TO BE PLENTY TOUGH.

HENRI PÉLISSIER (FAR RIGHT) IN THE MIDDLE OF ONE OF HIS PATENTED WITHDRAWS.

HENRI PÉLISSIER & CO.

A POSTER FROM AUTOMOTO BICYCLES TOUTS ITS BIKE TEAM, AS TEAM LEADER HENRI PÉLISSIER BECAME THE FIRST FRENCHMAN TO WIN THE TOUR SINCE 1911 AND ITALIAN RUNNER-UP OTTAVIO BOTTECCHIA SHOWED HIMSELF TO BE THE STAR OF THE FUTURE.

AN EXHAUSTED PÉLISSIER AFTER WINNING HIS FIRST TOUR DE FRANCE STAGE. THE OLDEST OF THE PÉLISSIERS MADE AN IMPRESSIVE TOUR DEBUT IN 1913, BUT HE WOULD HAVE TO WAIT UNTIL AFTER WORLD WAR I TO CEMENT HIS PLACE AT THE TOP.

The Pélissier clan—Henri, Charles, and Francis— goes down in cycling history as the greatest family to have ever raced bicycles. Combined, they won virtually all the great races of their day.

Of the trio, however, it was only Henri, the oldest, who managed to win the Tour de France. And considering his long list of victories, it is surprising that Pélissier only won the race once. But then, his biggest obstacle in the Tour came not from the terrain, but from race director Henri Desgrange, and their more-hate-than-love relationship provided plenty of fodder for the press. Both the cyclist and organizer possessed strong egos. As a result, their relationship remained a bullish standoff.

Freudians might have claimed that Pélissier's intolerance of the didactic Desgrange stemmed from earlier problems with his own father, who attempted to prevent him from cycling. But

Pélissier did not go in for such intellectual analysis, and any problems he had he preferred to settle on the road. To Pélissier, Desgrange was a tyrant— nothing more, nothing less.

For Desgrange, however, everyone submitted to the law of the Tour, and no rider, no matter how great, could threaten to usurp the race's supreme spot in the sport. When he threatened Pélissier with penalties in the 1921 Tour, Pélissier simply stopped, knocked on the door of a local to ask for a drink, and cruised in well behind the leaders. "I'm not a number. I'm a free man!" he grunted before quitting the race.

In 1922, with the yellow jersey on his shoulders, Pélissier again quit due to one of Desgrange's rulings. "Your Tour de France doesn't impress us [the Pélissier brothers] any more than any other race," he shot at Desgrange.

In 1923, perhaps for no other reason than to justify his criticisms of Desgrange, Pélissier vowed to go the Tour's distance. It was a good decision: he took the overall victory and flaunted it at Desgrange like a slap in the face.

Pélissier was now clearly on top of his game, and among professional cyclists he was the unspoken boss of the bunch. Such a position of power offered him considerable influence in the Tour de France. But in 1924, he again was butting egos with race officials, and his mark on the race was one of disgust rather than of glory.

Pélissier habitually changed jerseys during long races, and as the weather warmed on the first stage of the 1924 Tour, he shed his long-sleeved wool jersey. But according to the rule book, such a move was a clear no-no. When a Tour official threatened to penalize Pélissier for the infraction,

BEFORE THE BIRTH OF THE DERAILLEUR, CHANGING GEARS WAS QUITE AN ORDEAL. HERE, TWO RIDERS TURN THE REAR WHEELS AROUND SO AS TO USE A SMALLER COG FOR THE DESCENT.

ONE TOUR RIDER TAKING A WATER STOP IN 1923.

Pélissier erupted. As soon as stage two started, he rode alongside his brother Francis and said it was time for them to pull out.

A journalist, Albert Londres, finally caught up to the Pélissiers in a roadside tavern, where the two brothers were holding court with the local fans. Londres's subsequent account of the brothers' experience, entitled "Slaves of the Road," immediately became part of Tour legend. It vividly and emotionally described the rigors, sacrifices, and exploitation of the cyclists. Certainly it was not the kind of story Desgrange wanted splashed across the front pages during his race. But then he

was the first to know that the Pélissiers were never ones to hide their feelings. After all, they were *hommes libres* (free men).

The next year Henri again dropped out early in the race. His heart was clearly no longer in the Tour, and he never signed up again, though Francis and Charles did continue to compete. Apparently, Henri's private life was just as volatile as his professional cycling career had been. In 1935, his name was again in the headlines for troubling reasons. In the midst of a heated argument with his lover, he was shot and killed. Henri, it seems, never was the kind to discuss things rationally.

1924–1925: OTTAVIO BOTTECCHIA'S SHOOTING STAR

WITH HIS LONG LEGS AND FLUID PEDAL STROKE, ITALY'S OTTAVIO BOTTECCHIA
IS STILL REMEMBERED AS ONE OF THE TOUR'S GREAT CLIMBERS.

Great champions are often compared to shooting stars. Their rise to the top can be spectacular and sudden, but their decline is often equally abrupt. But of all the cometlike careers in the history of cycling, few were more brilliant—or brief—than that of Italy's Ottavio Bottecchia. Almost any conversation about the charismatic but enigmatic Italian begins with his shocking and ambiguous death in 1927 on the roadside during a routine training ride.

Bottecchia was born to ride, and it certainly must be symbolic that this one-time mason used a bicycle to repeatedly escape from his German captors during World War I. After the war Bottecchia abandoned bricklaying to become a professional cyclist. French champion Henri Pélissier saw him ride in the 1922 Tour of Lombardy and immediately hired him for an assault on the Tour de France in 1923.

Bottecchia wasn't pretty to look at—he was too short in the torso and too long in the legs—but a natural-born climber like Bottecchia could only be a strong ally for Pélissier in the mountains of the Tour de France. It proved a wise move. Pélissier won the race with key support from Bottecchia, who finished a promising second. And in the eyes of many, the little-known Italian stole the show. Even the hard-to-please race director, Henri Desgrange, called him "the most sensational revelation of the Tour."

Certainly Pélissier was happy to have Bottecchia riding as a friend rather than a foe. "He might look like a peasant," Pélissier said, "but, oh, how he can climb. He's pure class." Pélissier was just one of many to predict a great future for the Italian.

In 1924 Bottecchia made it clear that he had come to the Tour with his own ambitions. He won the opening stage, took the yellow jersey, and never let go of it. "The Mason from Frioul" won that year's race with such ease that other Tour riders could only look on in amazement.

"Trying to follow Bottecchia in the mountains is rather like suicide," bemoaned the 1924 runner-up, Nicolas Frantz. "He climbs with such persistent power that, after a moment, if you try to follow him, you'd be asphyxiated." Frantz finished over thirty-five minutes behind Bottecchia.

Bottecchia's victory made him the first Italian Tour winner, a feat he repeated in 1925 with similar ease. As in 1924, he powered his victory with four stage wins along the way. But already life at the top was taking its toll on Bottecchia. After his 1925 win, he threatened to never return. Putting the hurt on the competition as he did was simply too tough on his body, Bottecchia claimed.

He did return to defend his title in 1926, but he was clearly not the same rider. In a fit of despair, he abandoned on the stage in the Pyrenees from Bayonne to Luchon—the same stage he used to humiliate his competition only twelve months earlier. Suddenly, only four years after turning professional, he retired from competition.

Then, just months after announcing his retirement, he was found dead, killed mysteriously on a training ride near his home in Frioul, Italy. Immediately, rumors surrounding his death began to swirl.

Initial reports recorded a natural death due to freak circumstances, but from the beginning suspicion arose. Politically, times were turbulent in Italy, and despite the international glory his victories brought to the rising Fascist party, Bottecchia was not a vocal supporter of his country's politics. After all, he was an athlete. He was paid to use his legs, not his mouth. And when he did open his mouth, he had a reputation for being less than tactful.

No real clues about his death emerged until twenty years later, when an Italian immigrant in America swore on his deathbed that he had murdered Bottecchia under contract with the Fascists. And in 1973, Don Dante Nigris, the priest who had issued the last sacraments to Bottecchia, seemed to confirm, on his own deathbed, that Fascists, humiliated by the successes of the independent champion, had indeed murdered Bottecchia.

Some, however, cling to another story that Bottecchia was killed by a local farmer who threw a rock at the cyclist for stealing grapes and accidentally struck a fatal blow.

But no matter the cause of his tragic end, Bottecchia is remembered as the first Italian winner of the Tour de France and as a real *campionissimo*, a true champion.

LES GLOIRES DU CYCLISME
BOTTECCHIA

DIX
PARIS

27

SOMETIMES COWS WERE THE ONLY SPECTATORS IN THE MOUNTAINS, AS IN THE 1922 RACE.

DEFENDING TOUR CHAMP NICOLAS FRANTZ DRIVES THE PACE DURING THE 1928 RACE.

1927—1929:
CH-CH-CH-CH-CHANGES

No Tour route could be too tough for race director Henri Desgrange. Or so it seemed. By 1927, the thrill of adding higher mountain peaks had lost its appeal, and Desgrange complained that the race lacked suspense. To shake it up, he abolished mass starts on the flat stages and instead required riders to start individually or with just their own teams.

This newfangled format reduced the tactical nature of racing in the pack, but it also made the race that much harder to endure. Without the shelter of the pack, weaker riders were soon exposed. Only the strongest made it to Paris. And, as if that weren't enough, these were also some of the longest Tours in the history of the event.

The changed format forged a new breed of Tour rider. In addition to climbing, the potential winner had to be strong in long distance pursuit riding, in which beating the clock was crucial. Every kilometer counted. New stars surfaced like Luxembourg's Nicolas Frantz. But nonstars like Belgium's Maurice DeWaele also exploited the sometimes lopsided nature of the new format.

In 1927, Frantz found himself thirty minutes behind Hector Martin of Belgium going into the Pyrenees. But with the help of his team, Frantz launched an all-night attack on the treacherous mountain roads. At the summit of the Col du Tourmalet, Martin was no longer a factor, and French hopeful André Leducq was fourteen minutes behind.

By the time the race returned to Paris, Frantz had little competition. Only 39 of the 142 starters managed to finish this excruciating endurance test. Some of the riders were so devastated that even the hard-headed Desgrange had to take pity. In an uncharacteristic fit of generosity, the big boss showed that he did have a heart after all. He went so far as to add a bench-squad system in 1928. Substitute riders were introduced, and teams were now able to replace exhausted riders midway through the race.

But Desgrange's new system still didn't even out the field. Instead, strong teams just got stronger, while weaker teams virtually collapsed under the strain.

In 1928, the revamped Alcyon squad, which was obviously the strongest, surged to the front in the opening stages and paved the way for a second victory for Frantz. After the Pyrenees, Frantz had a forty-one-minute lead. He did have a brief scare near the end of the race when he broke his front fork, but not even technical troubles could get in the way of the Alcyon team. Frantz's teammates waited for him and organized a long frantic chase that helped him cut his losses and save the yellow jersey by a mere two minutes.

By 1929, Desgrange's new team concept was a flagrant flop.

Again the Alcyon team was the strongest. The problem was that their new leader, Maurice DeWaele, was not. Although he managed to grab the yellow jersey, by the time the race hit the Alps, the Belgian chief fell ill. With the possibility of defeat looming, the Alcyons redefined the meaning of team work. Teammates took turns surrounding DeWaele, virtually pushing him over climbs, while others formed a formidable road block at the front of the pack, slowing its pace and thwarting any breakaways. DeWaele saved his shirt, but he lost all respect. And Desgrange was so outraged that he angrily disposed of the team-time-trial concept. Without the element of chance, there was even less suspense.

1930–1939: THE TOUR TURNS NATIONALISTIC

ANTONIN MAGNE ON THE ATTACK ON THE FINAL STAGE OF THE 1938 TOUR. SOON HE WOULD BE JOINED BY HIS TEAMMATE AND COMPATRIOT ANDRÉ LEDUCQ, AND THE TWO HEROES WOULD FINISH THE STAGE ARM-IN-ARM.

SOME THINGS NEVER CHANGE. CHECKING OUT THE MORNING'S HEADLINES HAS ALWAYS BEEN A FAVORITE PASTIME AMONG TOUR RIDERS BEFORE THE START.

After the 1929 Tour, Henri Desgrange swore revenge. Desgrange felt that the Tour was being held hostage by the team-time-trial format. After the unimpressive win by the sick and injured Maurice DeWaele, Desgrange, never one to mince his words, blurted, "How could the riders let a cadaver like that win?"

Always the purist, he pointed his finger at the top commercial sponsors, whose teams controlled the race. But he seemed to forget that only three years earlier he had brainstormed the team-time-trial idea himself. Little matter. Desgrange abruptly introduced another new idea: national teams. And his latest brainstorm worked.

One hundred riders, divided into eight-man national teams, started the 1930 race with France, Italy, Belgium, Germany, and Spain topping the bill. Additional teams would be added in ensuing years, and this national racing format lasted until 1968.

Certainly nobody was happier than the French. For the first time since before World War I, they flourished in their national tour, and riders like Charles Pélissier and André Leducq became national heroes.

The youngest of the Pélissier brothers took the yellow jersey on the opening stage of the 1930 race. But then he had little choice. His older brothers, Henri and Francis, had both worn the yellow jersey, and family pride obliged little Charly to do the same. Pélissier went on to win eight stages, but he was also the first to admit that he was no match for the mountains. His teammate, Leducq, picked up the slack in the Pyrenees and went on to take top prize at the finish in Paris.

THE FIRST PUBLICITY CARAVAN The creation of national teams presented new problems to the race organizers. With the abolishment of commercially sponsored teams, Tour organizers needed new ways to bring money to the race. Desgrange had an idea. Tapping into the new advertising market, he created the first publicity caravans. Sponsors would fund part of the Tour and in return, their products would be advertised and distributed free along the Tour's route.

Such far-fetched advertising schemes, however, met with tepid response in socialist France. Just three sponsors went along for the ride during the first year. Soon, though, the key to commercial success became clear—food. The French love their food, and any sponsor offering culinary fare would get their share of attention.

It came as little surprise that the most popular sponsor that first year was the Menier chocolate producer, whose saccharine goodies were eagerly gobbled up by fans along the route.

TONIN TAKES OVER Leducq and Pélissier eventually had to make room for Antonin Magne. At the start of the 1931 race, Leducq was clearly not in shape to repeat. But since all the country's best rode on the same team, there was never a lack of leaders. Magne got the nod as the team's chief.

49

EVEN THE TOUR DE FRANCE, THE COUNTRY'S GREAT ESCAPE, COULD NOT AVOID THE MENACE OF WORLD WAR II. DURING THE STAGE FROM PARIS TO LILLE IN 1937, FRENCH TROOPS PRACTICING MILITARY MANEUVERS TAKE A BREAK TO WATCH THE TOUR PASS.

Magne faced strong competition from Italian climber Antonio Pesenti and Belgium hopeful Jef Demuysère. But thanks to his fans, Magne held on to win his first Tour. As predicted, Magne made his move early, with a big attack in the Pyrenees, and on the Pau-Luchon stage he finished seven minutes in front of Demuysère. The Belgian, however, was waiting for more familiar terrain. And he just might have upset Magne if the Frenchman hadn't received a tip.

Magne enjoyed reading letters from his family during the Tour, but never fan mail. It was bad luck, he thought. Toward the end of the 1931 race, however, an oversized letter caught his eye. Despite his superstition, he opened it to find a detailed account of the racing strategy to be used by the Belgian challenger. The fan said he'd recently visited Demuysère's hometown and had overheard that the Belgian was planning a surprise attack over the cobbled roads of northern France.

Magne could not afford to ignore the information. Demuysère was only twelve minutes and fifty-six seconds behind—not much in the days when riders had to tend to their own breakdowns. On the stage between Charleville and Malo-les-Bains, the Frenchman watched the Belgian. And sure enough, Demuysère attacked just as the letter said he would. But when he did, Magne was ready. Demuysère finished the stage seventeen minutes out in front—with Magne glued to his wheel. From then on, the Frenchman was less superstitious when it came to reading his mail.

Magne and Leducq each went on to win another Tour, and the French team so dominated the thirties that lesser team riders like Georges Speicher and Roger Lapébie also had time to win their own Tours. For the French at least, this period goes down as the belle époque.

AFTER YEARS OF DOMINATION BY THE FRENCH, GINO BARTALI'S 1938 VICTORY ANNOUNCED A NEW ITALIAN ERA. UNFORTUNATELY IT WOULD HAVE TO WAIT UNTIL AFTER WORLD WAR II TO BE CONTINUED.

THE TOUR IS MORE THAN JUST A BIKE RACE. THIS 1934 POSTER ANNOUNCES A MUSICAL PARADE CELEBRATING THE TOP CYCLISTS AND ILLUSTRATES HOW DEEPLY THE TOUR WAS ROOTED IN THE FRENCH IMAGINATION.

WITH THE INTRODUCTION OF NATIONAL TEAMS, THE TOUR DE FRANCE COULD NO LONGER RELY ON THE BIKE TEAM SPONSORS TO FOOT THE BILL. ALONG WITH THE PUBLICITY CARAVAN, NUMEROUS COMPANIES OUTSIDE THE SPORT USED THE TOUR AS A VEHICLE FOR ADVERTISING CAMPAIGNS. GRAF, A PROCESSED SWISS CHEESE, LIKENED THEIR ROUND CONTAINERS TO BICYCLE WHEELS.

Dédiée au journal L'Auto et aux coureurs du "Tour de France"

Les "Tour de France"
1934

Chanson roulante créée par **PERCHICOT** pour entraîner les Géants de la route

 G. SPEICHER
 R. LAPÉBIE
 R. LOUVIOT
 ANT. MAGNE
 CH. PÉLISSIER

 R. LE GREVES
 M. ARCHAMBAUD
 G. REBRY
 FR. BONDUEL
 E. DE CALUWÉ

 R. GIJSSELS
 J. MARTANO
 F. BATTESINI
 K. STOEPEL
 A. BUCHI

 V. TRUEBA
 L. MONTERO
 Y. LE GOFF
 J. BIDOT
 H. BUSE
Photos Meurisse

L. ROELS	L. HARDIQUEST	R. MAES	Fr. DICTUS	BERGAMASCHI	FOLCO
GESTRI	CAZZULANI	GOTTI	VIGNOLI	MEINI	FRANZIL	MOLINAR	MORELLI
W. BLATTMANN	K. STETTLER	Aug. ERNE	M. CANARDO	Fr. EZQUERRA	L. GEYER
W. KUTZBACH	R. WOLKE	K. NITSCHKE	R. RISCH	B. WOLKE	R. VIETTO

Pour Piano et Chant, 6 fr.   Pour Chant seul, 1.50

Paroles de   Musique de
Léo LELIÈVRE fils   Jean BOYER

ÉDITIONS SALABERT ▪ PARIS

Vente en Gros : 22, Rue Chauchat, Paris-9e

HOMMAGE DE L'ÉDITEUR

ONE FEMALE FAN SPLASHES ITALY'S FIORENZO MAGNI AS HE CLIMBS BY IN THE 1934 RACE.

AFTER THE TEAM WON SEVEN TOURS, ALCYON BICYCLES USED ANDRÉ LEDUCQ'S SECOND TOUR VICTORY FOR AN ADVERTISING CAMPAIGN. ACCORDING TO THE POSTER, "IN ORDER TO BUILD A GOOD BICYCLE IT IS ESSENTIAL TO PARTICIPATE IN RACES LIKE ALCYON HAS DONE FOR THIRTY YEARS." AND AFTER ALCYON WON SEVEN TOURS, FEW WOULD ARGUE THAT THE FRAME BUILDERS DID NOT KNOW HOW TO MAKE A GOOD BIKE.

DEFENDING CHAMPION GEORGES SPEICHER COLLAPSES AFTER THE FINISH INTO AIX-LES-BAINS IN 1933. WITH VIRTUALLY NO CHANCE OF A REPEAT VICTORY, SPEICHER IS ONCE AGAIN REDUCED TO THE ROLE OF TEAM RIDER ON THE POWERFUL FRENCH TEAM.

VIETTO, THE SENTIMENTAL STAR OF THE 1934 TOUR, HAPPILY GIVES HIS AUTOGRAPH TO AN ATTRACTIVE FAN.

RENÉ VIETTO: THEY CALLED HIM "THE KING"

ON THE PORTET D'ASPET CLIMB, KING RENÉ SITS ON A WALL AND WEEPS AFTER SACRIFICING HIS FRONT WHEEL FOR HIS TEAM LEADER DURING THE 1934 RACE.

Bicycle racing has two kinds of winners: those who win races and those who win our hearts. René Vietto didn't win many races, but in the category of hearts he was the king. In fact, that's what they called him—King René.

His nickname came not from his exploits but from his sacrifices, which made him even more of a hero in the eyes of his fans. Two-time Tour winner Antonin Magne certainly didn't dispute the merit of Vietto's nickname. After all, if Vietto hadn't been around, Magne would have lost the 1934 Tour.

In 1934, Vietto made his Tour debut, and what a debut it was. He dominated in the Alps. On the stage from Aix-les-Bains to Grenoble, the twenty-year-old rode far from the race favorites for a long solo victory. At one point he was even in a position to take the yellow jersey from Magne. But Magne was the leader of the French national team, and

Vietto was not about to forget his designated role. He may have been the revelation of the race, but he remained a team worker. Such is the unspoken law of the peloton, and Vietto was not about to challenge it. Twice Magne needed a wheel change in the Pyrenees, and twice Vietto gave up his wheel—and his chances. If the flat tires had occurred in other parts of the race, perhaps other teammates would have been called upon. But in the mountains there *were* no other teammates.

On the Col de Portet d'Aspet, Vietto even doubled back and climbed up a mountain to aid his leader in distress. "Heck, if I hadn't given Magne that wheel, he'd still be stuck on the mountain," he said with his characteristic sarcasm long after the race had finished.

His self-sacrifice certainly cost him the Tour, but it also captured the hearts of his compatriots. For many he remained the sentimental winner. And anyway, other Tours seemed destined for Vietto. But World War II and the arrival of a certain Gino Bartali forever sealed Vietto's fate.

In the 1947 Tour, the first postwar race, Vietto appeared to have discovered a second youth. He grabbed the yellow jersey in the Alps, and many thought he would keep it to the end. But the stage nineteen time trial dashed his chances. He cracked midway through the race—perhaps after taking a few shots of turned cider—and fell from first to fifth place.

No, Vietto would never win the Tour—just our hearts.

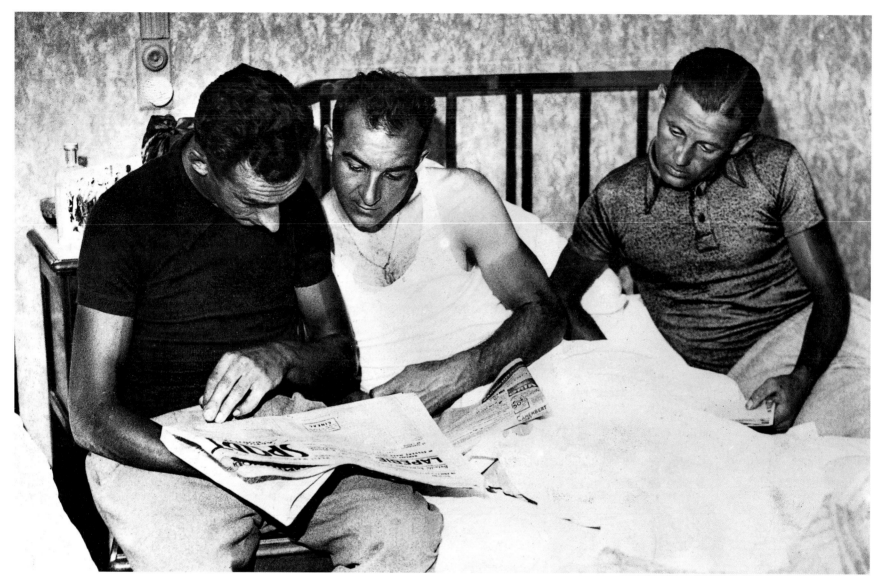

DURING THE 1937 RACE EVENTUAL WINNER ROGER LAPÉBIE (CENTER) SCANS THE SPORTS PAGE WHILE RESTING IN BED.

THIS DAMSEL SEEMS UNDISTRESSED BY GINO BARTALI'S MUD-CAKED FACE AS SHE SMOOCHES THE ITALIAN CHAMPION AT THE STAGE FINISH IN STRASBOURG IN 1938. BARTALI WENT ON TO WIN.

POST—WORLD WAR II AND BEYOND

IF THE TOUR WAS LIKE GOLIATH, LITTLE JEAN ROBIC WAS ITS DAVID. ROBIC WASN'T THE MOST IMPRESSIVE TOUR WINNER, BUT POST—WORLD WAR II FRANCE LOVED HIS PUNCHY RESISTANCE. MOREOVER, DURING THE 1947 TOUR, THE NEWLYWED ROBIC WANTED TO OFFER HIS YOUNG BRIDE AN EXTRASPECIAL WEDDING PRESENT.

COPPI AND BARTALI RIDING AND WRITING HISTORY ON THE IZOARD PASS IN 1949. NO MATCH FOR HIS YOUNG COUNTRYMAN, BARTALI BARGAINED FOR THE STAGE WIN AND LATER HELPED COPPI WIN HIS FIRST TOUR.

Few periods in bicycle racing are remembered with more fondness than the one following World War II. Postwar Europe was in disarray, and in an effort to start over, people were identifying with various "isms." Socialism, communism, and capitalism headed the list in this idealistic period.

Cycling had its share of "isms," too: Bartali-ism and Coppi-ism, to name just two. But then, what would one expect from a sport that the French refer to as cycl-"isme"?

In an era drained of its heroes, fans latched onto cycling's top riders. For some, athletes were the only real heroes that remained. An athlete, at least, was free of political and social baggage.

That is not to say that certain riders did not appeal to specific audiences. Italians love their rivalries in sports, and they have often pitted one *campionissimo*, or champion, against another. During the 1940s and 1950s the country was virtually split between the "Coppi-ists" and the "Bartali-ists." Gino Bartali,

a salt-of-the-earth devout Catholic, was the rural hero. The stylish Fausto Coppi, despite his own rural upbringing, appealed to the new increasingly urban generation.

In France, fans rallied around the powerful French national team in the 1950s. Stars like Louison Bobet, Raphaël Geminiani, and André Darrigade became national heroes. Later, a division of sentiments similar to the Coppi-Bartali contest in Italy would develop in the 1960s between country-bred Raymond Poulidor and the suave Jacques Anquetil. Although Anquetil won five Tours de France, he never managed to match Poulidor in the popularity polls.

Throughout this postwar period, the Tour de France's popularity exploded. Admittedly, part of the boom was due to French minister Léon Blum, who, just before the start of the war, established mandatory annual vacation time in France. As a result, hoards of French workers hit the road—half the country in July, the other half in August—and suddenly the Tour had a captive

audience. For the French, watching the Tour pass simply became part of the rites of summer.

ITALIAN RENAISSANCE: BARTALI AND COPPI RIDE AND WRITE TOUR LEGEND
When Italian Gino Bartali returned to the Tour in 1948, many wondered whether the aging champion could still dominate. Bartali had won the Tour in 1938, but that was a decade and a whole world war ago. And after he lost the Tour of Italy in May, many simply thought *il vecchio*, the old one, was washed up. But resurrection time came in July.

Bartali instantly grabbed the yellow jersey on the opening stage. Knowing he could not defend it throughout the three-week affair, he let the Tour's young, feisty riders fight for glory during the first week. Among these neophytes was French rider Louison Bobet, who won stage six to Biarritz.

Bartali simply waited for the mountains, where he could exploit his specialty—climbing. Even after all those years, his accelerations in the mountains

LIKE MANY BELGIAN RACERS, ROGER GHYSELINOK WAS NO FAN OF THE HEAT. ON THE STAGE FROM ROUEN TO ST. MALO DURING THE 1949 TOUR, HE DOES HIS BEST TO STAY HYDRATED. BUT WATER ALONE DID NOT SUFFICE, AND GHYSELINOK NEVER FINISHED THE RACE.

remained vicious. Justifying another of his nicknames, *il pio* (the pious), he won the first Pyrenees mountain stage to the Catholic pilgrimage town of Lourdes. Perhaps Gino's habit of eating with a religious statuette on the table was paying off. And Bartali kept on winning. He stamped his name on the following stage into Toulouse, and then in the Alps, he was simply unbeatable. He won every Alpine stage—Briançon, Aix-les-Bains, and Lausane—and rode to victory in Paris.

THE LEGENDARY LINE Bartali entered the 1949 Tour prepared to defend his title. But tagging along with the Italian team was a certain Fausto Coppi. Among his compatriots, Coppi had become a legend—by 1949 he had already won the Giro

d'Italia three times. Nevertheless, Coppi's Tour de France potential remained unknown.

Coppi appeared doomed early in the 1949 Tour, as crashes and mechanical mishaps cost him dearly in the opening week. But in the Pyrenees he made up for lost time and was soon within reach of the lead.

From the start of the first stage in the Alps, between Cannes and Briançon, the Bartali-Coppi duo dominated. By now, however, the energetic Coppi was clearly the strongest, and he was hungry to finally win a Tour. On the climb over the grueling Izoard pass, Bartali was struggling, and Coppi announced, "Now, Gino, I'm going." Bartali bargained: "Let's finish together! Today I'm thirty-five years old. Let me win the stage. Tomorrow you will

win the Tour." The cool Coppi still had room for a little chivalry, and the pact was made: Bartali won in Briançon.

Then, on the following stage from Briançon to Aoste, Bartali honored his word; Coppi raced toward the stage finish in Aoste, Italy, alone. Three stages later, Coppi cemented his hold on the yellow jersey by winning the final time trial, and the Tour was his.

COPPI DRIVES UP THE IZOARD DURING HIS MAGIC 1949 TOUR.

COPPI'S BACK! DESPITE THE SWISS INTERLUDE IN 1950 AND 1951, THE ITALIAN RETURNED IN 1952. AND TO SHOW THAT HE WAS ONCE AGAIN AT THE HEIGHT OF THE SPORT, HE WON EVERY MOUNTAIN-TOP STAGE FINISH DURING THE RACE.

NEITHER RAIN NOR SLEET STOPS THE TOUR DE FRANCE. AND SOMETIMES NEITHER DO TRAINS.
HERE JEAN "LEATHER HEAD" ROBIC LEADS THE CHARGE OVER THE BARRIERS.

ALWAYS STYLISH, COPPI STEALS A FEW
SECONDS TO SPONGE OFF DURING THE
PROTOCOL CEREMONIES.

LIKE MANY CHAMPIONS, FAUSTO COPPI WAS
ALSO QUITE THE ACROBAT ON THE BIKE.

SWISS STARS FERDI KUBLER (LEFT) AND HUGO KOBLET (RIGHT) CHAT DURING A DOWN MOMENT OF THE 1951 TOUR. THE TWO RIDERS MAY HAVE HAD DISTINCTLY DIFFERENT PERSONALITIES, BUT FOR A FEW YEARS AT LEAST, THE BRUTISH KUBLER AND THE DAPPER KOBLET SHARED THE SPOTLIGHT OF INTERNATIONAL CYCLING. THEIR COUNTRYMEN ARE STILL TRYING TO MATCH THEIR FEATS.

1950–1951: SWISS INTERLUDE

After the great rivalry between Italians Fausto Coppi and Gino Bartali, the Swiss took over with their own historic duo: Ferdi Kubler and Hugo Koblet. Koblet, like Coppi, was the aristocrat, while Kubler embodied Bartali's working-class spirit.

In his demeanor, Kubler appeared more Latin than Swiss. His emotions never strayed far from the surface, and he could easily break into a frustrated tirade when racing failed to fall in his favor. When racing did go his way—like it did during the 1950 Tour de France—Kubler steamrolled his competition. Injuries and bad luck kept the top two Italian riders from contending in 1950: defending champion Coppi sat on the sidelines with a fractured pelvis, and veteran Gino Bartali crashed in the Pyrenees, losing his chance for the overall win.

Kubler, in contrast, was having the ride of his life. He took the lead on the flat stages after the Pyrenees and seemed to get stronger with each passing day. The French team battled ceaselessly, but they were no match for the emotional Swiss rider. It proved to be his only Tour triumph, but Kubler holds the rare distinction of being one of the only riders in Tour de France history to win the green points jersey (in 1954, when he finished second overall)—which is usually reserved for sprint specialists—as well as the yellow leader's jersey.

BARTALI EXITS IN FURY Gino Bartali was riding well in the 1950 Tour. He won the opening stage in the Pyrenees and claimed the yellow jersey. On the second mountain stage, however, he was knocked down by a drunken mob. Several of the fans poked Bartali and insulted him, and at one point someone flashed a knife in his face.

Bartali's teammate Fiorenzo Magni took over the lead at the end of the stage, but Bartali was still seething over the violence. That night he called a press conference and announced that the Italian team was withdrawing. The next morning, no one was wearing a yellow jersey in the race.

Swiss rider Ferdi Kubler inherited it two days later, by default.

KOBLET, KUBLER'S ANTITHESIS After Ferdi Kubler, the Swiss produced Hugo Koblet. He was the James Dean of cycling—unfortunately in more ways than one. Like Dean, Koblet was a natural. Efforts that brought other cyclists to their knees hardly solicited a wince from Koblet. And while others gasped across the finish line, Koblet could be seen suavely pulling a comb from his jersey pocket to resculpt his hair before meeting with fans and journalists. Now *that's* style.

Like Kubler, his Swiss predecessor, Koblet had a knack for inconsistency. But when he found his form, there was no stopping him.

The legendary Fausto Coppi looked like a second-rank rider next to Koblet during the 1951 Tour. Koblet came to the Tour de France and humiliated the *crème de la crème* of world cycling. He won everything: time-trial stages, mountain stages, and flat stages. He even amused himself by soloing off the front and dangling ahead of the hard-chasing peloton. The competition was so crushed that his closest challenger, France's Raphaël Geminiani, said, "If there were two Koblets, I'd change professions." Geminiani finished twenty-two minutes behind Koblet when the race returned to Paris.

But Koblet's virtuosity was delicate. Only months after his Tour victory he contracted a mysterious venereal disease while riding in an exhibition race in Mexico. Although the disease did not appear to be serious, he never completely recovered. Suddenly the champion who once floated up mountains struggled over the climbs. His once-fluid pedal stroke had turned blocklike. He never finished another Tour de France and retired prematurely in 1956.

Life after cycling provided even less promise. By the early 1960s, Koblet was heavily in debt and suffering from marital problems when he crashed his white Alfa Romeo sports car into a tree at over one hundred kilometers an hour. He died four days later, but the cause of the accident still remains unknown. There were no skid marks to offer any visible sign of braking, and suicide is suspected.

But then reconversion from professional sports is filled with failures. Everyday life sometimes just doesn't stand up to the highs attainable in sports. And perhaps the Swiss star simply submitted to his own disillusionment.

AFTER PASSING HIS RIVAL IN THE TIME TRIAL, FERDI KUBLER LOOKS BACK AT THE GRIMACING RAPHAËL GEMINIANI BEFORE STORMING TO VICTORY. AFTER STARTING SIX MINUTES IN FRONT OF THE KUBLER, "GEM" IS VISIBLY HUMILIATED. BUT THEN HE WOULD HAVE TO GET USED TO TAKING A BEATING FROM SWISS RIDERS.

FLYING LIKE AN AIRPLANE, HUGO KOBLET DRAGS FAUSTO COPPI UP A CLIMB IN THE PYRENEES DURING THE 1951 TOUR. IN THE YEAR OF KOBLET'S MAGICAL MYSTERY TOUR, EVEN THE LEGENDARY ITALIAN SUBMITTED TO THE PULL OF THE CHARISMATIC SWISS STAR.

FERDI KUBLER WITH JUST ONE OF THE MANY BOUQUETS HE WON IN THE 1950 TOUR.

SIMPLY LOUISON: FROM BAKER'S SON TO FRENCH ICON

AFTER BOBET'S REIGN, CLIMBERS LIKE FEDERICO BAHAMONTÉS (RIGHT) AND CHARLY GAUL (LEFT) TOOK CENTER STAGE IN THE TOUR.

Louis "Louison" Bobet was just the kind of hero that France had been looking for. The post–World War II years had been tough on French cycling fans. Every year their national Tour was stolen by Italian or Swiss riders—if not Bartali then Coppi, if not Kubler then Koblet. Only the 1947 victory by the little-known Jean Robic provided any respite. Robic, however, was not exactly the most charismatic of champions, and his win soon became a footnote in Tour history.

Then came Bobet. He brought an end to the foreign cycling invasion, but just as important, he did so with style. Although he was the son of a baker from Brittany (in the northwestern region of France), on a bike he was considered an aristocrat because of his undeniable strength.

In France they call it *classe*. And when the term is applied to cyclists, it refers not only to a rider's raw talent but also to his efficient style of riding. Such riders give the impression that they were simply born to pedal. Louis Bobet, or Louison, as he was commonly called, had just that kind of *classe*. And his reign at the top of the cycling world was one of the great eras of French cycling.

From the day he made the French national team in 1947, Bobet left his humble beginnings as a baker's son behind. In his first Tour (1948), Bobet won a stage, challenged Italian legend Gino Bartali in the mountains, and briefly captured the yellow jersey. It was simply a matter of time before Bobet would take the overall honors—or so it seemed.

The wait was longer than expected. After Bartali and Coppi, Switzerland's Kubler and Koblet had their say in the Tour de France. But when Bobet finally did carry the yellow jersey to Paris, he did it convincingly. From 1953 to 1955 he topped the Tour de France charts. And although Philippe Thys had already become a three-time Tour winner, Bobet added the word consecutive to the feat.

Bobet possessed an uncanny ability to come back from the brink of disaster—the acid test of a true champion. In the 1948 Tour, Bobet suffered from a foot infection and many expected him to abandon. His response, however, was a long solo attack and a stage win on the roads from San Remo (in Italy) to Cannes.

In 1955 Bobet suffered from saddle sores, and he lost precious time in the Alps. Rumors spread, and critics predicted he would falter on the dreaded stage over Mont Ventoux. But it was Bobet's competition that faltered under the torrid pace he set on the "giant of Provence." At the stage finish in Avignon, after a solo attack, Bobet took back the lead.

But if Bobet is remembered as one of the century's great cyclists, it is not simply because he won three Tours. By the time he retired in 1962, Bobet had built one of the most complete victory lists any champion cyclist will ever produce. In addition to his Tour triple, Bobet also collected the most enviable classics. Of cycling's monuments, Bobet won all five: Milan–San Remo, the Tour of Flanders, the Tour of Lombardy, Paris-Roubaix, and the 1954 World Championship.

When an auto accident brought an end to his competitive career, he became a successful businessman, opening a string of saltwater health spas.

THE LEGENDARY LOUISON BOBET WON HIS THIRD TOUR IN 1955 WITH A CLUTCH SOLO ATTACK ON THE DAUNTING MONT VENTOUX CLIMB.

THERE IS NOTHING LIKE A SPLASH UNDER THE HOSE TO BEAT SUMMER'S HEAT.

JACQUES ANQUETIL: A CAREER IN OVERDRIVE

ANQUETIL AFTER WINNING HIS FIRST TOUR IN 1957.

ANQUETIL'S LAST STAND. "MASTER JACQUES" BIDS FAREWELL TO THE TOUR IN 1966.

He was only seventeen years old when he won his first Grand Prix des Nations, then the unofficial World Championships for time trialing. And seventeen years later, when he finally retired, Jacques Anquetil closed the book on one of the richest careers the sport of cycling has ever known.

For most of those seventeen years, Anquetil lived and raced as though he was a breed apart. Anquetil embodied perfection on a bicycle, and, appropriately, he turned professional with a team named "La Perle" (the pearl).

Although he came from the country, Anquetil embodied the hip look of 1950s Paris. Cruising in his sports car to numerous races—his platinum blond wife, Janine, never far from his side—Anquetil broke all the old-school rules. Because of his lavish lifestyle, critics slayed him. They claimed he would burn out prematurely, and at first their predictions almost came true. After winning his first Tour in 1957, Anquetil struggled for four years before repeating. But then Master Jacques silenced all his critics by becoming the first five-time Tour de France winner.

Anquetil sealed his five Tour de France victories with his stunning time-trialing skills, yet in the mountains he rarely took the initiative. In the 1990s another champion, Spain's Miguel Indurain,

would carbon copy Anquetil's formula. He, too, would win five Tours de France.

For Anquetil, time trialing became a virtual fetish, and it remained the root of all his greatest successes. In addition to the numerous races against the clock he captured during the Tour de France, he won the prestigious Grand Prix des Nations time trial nine times.

That is not to say that the blond-haired, blue-eyed star never suffered on the bike. He suffered plenty—like the time he overindulged in a lamb roast on the rest day of the 1964 Tour. Indigestion the next day in the Pyrenees nearly cost him his fifth Tour de France title. He immediately fell off the pace once the road started to climb, but according to legend, Anquetil's remedy came in the form of a couple of swigs of champagne—a last-ditch effort from his team director, Raphaël Geminiani. It worked, and Anquetil battled back to finish with the leaders at the end of the stage. Although Anquetil was known to suffer, like the handful of champions that have dominated the sport, he always possessed the ability to shift into overdrive, a gear his opponents could rarely achieve.

Despite his calculated style of riding, his lifestyle was anything but conventional. Unlike his peers, Anquetil never seemed to follow any special diets

or training regimes, and his weakness for whiskey and cigarettes was well known. Once suited up and ready to race, however, Anquetil quickly shed his playboy image. In the years that Anquetil raced as a professional, he continually proved why he was the master. In 1956 he broke Fausto Coppi's legendary fourteen-year-old world hour record. And in a feat that defied age, he broke the record again, eleven years later. That performance, however, never made it into the record books, because Anquetil refused to submit to a drug-control test.

But then Anquetil was never a big fan of the antidrug movement in sports. Around the world Elvis was singing "I'm going to do it my way," and Anquetil, it seemed, was following the King's advice. Like the Pélissier brothers in the 1920s, Anquetil was first and foremost an *homme libre*. He once even discounted drug testing by saying, "You can't ride the Tour de France on mineral water."

Anquetil's fast-lane life caught up to him after he retired. Reports of his health problems echoed throughout the 1970s, and in 1987 Anquetil died of stomach cancer—less than twenty years after retiring from racing.

IN THIS RACE OF ATTRITION, THE RACE FOR WATER HAS ALWAYS BEEN CRITICAL.

A DAY IN THE COUNTRY TAKES ON A DISTINCTLY DIFFERENT TONE AMONG TOUR RIDERS. HERE ANDRÉ DARRIGADE (RIGHT) GRABS A DISCARDED UMBRELLA FROM THE ROADSIDE AND SHELTERS "MASTER JACQUES" FROM THE RAYS.

SHOWDOWN ON THE VOLCANO. FOR MOST OF THE CLIMB UP THE PUY DE DÔME, ANQUETIL (LEFT) BLUFFED POULIDOR (RIGHT) BY RIDING NEXT TO HIM. IT WORKED. WHEN POULIDOR FINALLY DID BREAK FREE IT WAS TOO LATE TO DO ANY SERIOUS DAMAGE.

1964: SHOWDOWN AT PUY DE DÔME

For many, 1964 was supposed to be the Tour for "Pou-Pou," popular French cyclist Raymond Poulidor. Since his Tour debut in 1963, the tough climber impressed critics and fans alike. That was the year he won the tough mountain stage from Briançon to Aix-les-Bains with his left wrist in a cast—the remnants of an earlier crash.

The next year he returned as the clear challenger to the supremacy of time-trial specialist Jacques Anquetil. Many, in fact, thought Anquetil's number was up. Once again he came to the race as the defending champion, but he arrived at the 1964 Tour clearly tired from his recent win in the Tour of Italy. And besides, what did another Tour victory mean? He had already become the first four-time winner. This time, his critics thought, his tendency to overextend himself would surely cost him the race.

After winning the stage-ten time trial and taking the lead, he assured that he was not far from his best form. So confident was Master Jacques that he happily gave up the coveted jersey during the ensuing stages. There was no need to waste himself defending the lead too early, especially when it seemed certain to return by the end of the race.

Perhaps it was with such confidence that Anquetil sauntered into a VIP picnic during the rest day in Andorra and feasted on a slab of roast lamb. When Poulidor attacked on the first climb the next morning, Anquetil was left in the barnyard. Because he immediately lost over four minutes to the leaders, Anquetil's Tour reign seemed over. Only a miraculous champagne-filled water bottle calmed his stomach troubles and after a long chase, he was back in the race.

Anquetil battled back to finish with the leaders, once again proving why he was the master. Poulidor, in contrast, suffered from a case of bad luck that would soon thwart his entire career. In the final kilometers he broke several spokes in his rear wheel and had to stop for a wheel change. Then, when his team mechanic gave him a push start with his new wheel, he crashed. Ironically Poulidor, the principal animator in this historic stage, would finish two minutes and thirty-six seconds behind.

A stubborn Poulidor bounced back by winning the following stage into Luchon. And throughout the rest of the Tour he dominated Anquetil in the mountains.

By the time the race reached the Puy de Dôme in the Massif Central—the final climb of the Tour—Anquetil held a mere fifty-six-second lead over Poulidor. The two climbed the ten-kilometer stretch up the bald peak of the now-defunct volcano side-by-side. It was a bluff move by Anquetil to show that he was just as strong. Eventually he did crack, and Poulidor immediately powered away in an effort to exploit his rival's weakness. But the calculated champion knew exactly what it would take to ensure his lead, and while he finished forty-two seconds behind Poulidor, he was still in the lead by fourteen seconds. The last stage, a time trial from Versailles to Paris, would easily be snapped up by Anquetil, still master in the race against the clock. He became the first five-time winner—with fifty-five minutes to spare.

1967: DEATH IN THE AFTERNOON

A STRICKEN TOM SIMPSON RECEIVES EMERGENCY AID ON THE ROCKS OF MONT VENTOUX, BUT MEDICS CAN DO NOTHING FOR HIM.

The 1967 Tour de France would be nearly forgettable if it were not for Tom Simpson. Raymond Poulidor was once again unable to capture the race, which seemed to have his name on it, and the eventual winner, Roger Pingeon, was easily footnoted into cycling's history. Although a solid rider, he was an uninspiring champion.

But Simpson, who did not finish the three-week race, would change the face of bike racing for decades to come. Simpson left his soul at the Tour de France when he collapsed and died on the brutal slopes of Mont Ventoux.

From the start, the 1967 Tour was known as one of the toughest routes of all time. It covered 4,780 kilometers and included both the Puy de Dôme and Mont Ventoux. On paper, the Tour was perfect for Poulidor, a superb climber. Unfortunately, organizers had reintroduced the national team structure that year, and the French team boasted many strong riders besides Poulidor, including 1966 winner Lucien Aimar and newcomer Roger Pingeon.

Organizers also added a new feature: a mini time trial called the Prologue that took place before the first stage. Poulidor jumped at the chance to make his mark early. On the Prologue he clocked one of the best times and looked set to take the yellow jersey.

Instead, it was French rider Pingeon who made a surprise attack on stage five from Roubaix to Jambes and grabbed nearly a six-minute lead from his rivals.

When Poulidor crashed while climbing the historic Ballon d'Alsace, he lost all hope of capturing the overall victory, and he decided to throw his support to Pingeon. Better an unpretentious up-and-comer than Lucien Aimar, the dubious defending champion, Poulidor thought.

But after stage thirteen, and that fateful trek to the summit of Mont Ventoux, no one thought about the yellow jersey.

Mont Ventoux instills fear and commands respect. Its 1,900-meter peak is not the highest in the Tour, but it poses unique problems to riders because the ascent begins near sea level. On the way up, riders often encounter soaring temperatures and a relentlessly steep climb that allows little time for recuperation. Unlike many mountain climbs, there are no flat switchbacks to allow a moment's respite. And the final six kilometers rise above the tree line through a lunarlike landscape that pits man against nature. Here, no rider is sheltered from the stiff winds and the hot rays of the sun.

Simpson collapsed three kilometers from the summit. Spectators helped him remount and continue, but he collapsed again, and doctors were unable to revive him.

Later, amphetamines were found in his body. Such performance-enhancing drugs were the fashionable choice of many cyclists during those years. They allowed Simpson to exceed his physical limits on the climb, but they prohibited his body from giving off its natural warning signals. Finally, his body simply shut down, and he collapsed from complete exhaustion. But by then it was too late.

Simpson represented the best of British cycling. He had won numerous classics and the 1965 World Championship. It took nearly twenty years for his country to produce another rider with as much talent. And for cycling in general, it was the end of an age of innocence. The next year the race was touted as the "clean" Tour. Even when he retired as the Tour's director, Jacques Goddet remembered the day Simpson died as the worst moment of his career.

Authorities could no longer close their eyes to drug use, but as the "Festina Affair" in the 1998 Tour would show, few lessons were learned from Simpson's sacrifice.

FRENCHMAN RAYMOND POULIDOR MADE A BIG SPLASH IN HIS FIRST
TOUR BY WINNING A STAGE AND FINISHING THIRD IN THE 1962 EDITION.

RAYMOND POULIDOR:
ONE FOR THE LOSERS

POULIDOR AFTER CRASHING IN THE 1968 TOUR, JUST ONE OF SEVERAL WRECKS THAT PROHIBITED HIM FROM EVER WINNING THE TOUR.

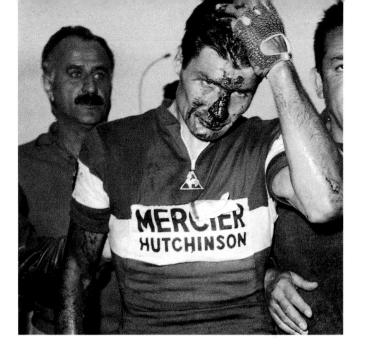

For every great champion, there is often a great loser. Victory, in the end, is judged in relation to its resulting defeats. But sometimes the losers, those who finally submit to a champion's wrath, also have their place in history. And perhaps no other Tour de France cyclist so embodied the dignity inherent in a heroic defeat as Raymond Poulidor.

"My big luck," he once said, "was to have lots of bad luck." And in the eyes of many, Poulidor wore his misfortune like a medal.

"Pou-Pou," as he was affectionately called, had the dubious honor of being outclassed by both Jacques Anquetil and Eddy Merckx, two of the century's greatest cyclists. On paper, it was in those years of Anquetil's decline, and before the dawning of the Merckx era, when insiders predicted that Poulidor would shine. But bad luck or bad tactics always seemed to get in the way.

At the end of nearly two decades of professional racing, however, Poulidor never once wore the yellow jersey. Winning the yellow jersey in the Tour of Spain was about as close as he came. But then, as everyone knows, the Spanish *amarillo* jersey is a far cry from the coveted *maillot jaune*.

No, Poulidor seemed to revel in the role of underdog. And in such a role he did win one category—that of the sentimental favorite. Anquetil, for all his talent, had too much of that existentialist chic style so fashionable in the early 1960s to ever hope to match Poulidor's simple salt-of-the-earth spirit. And if Anquetil stupefied onlookers with his nearly inhuman domination, Poulidor seemed to be the mirror of mortality, full of the failures and setbacks so abundant in everyday life.

Poulidor's popularity began in the 1963 Tour when he finished an astonishing third, despite starting the race with a cast on his left wrist. Soon France was divided into two camps, "Poulidoristes" and "Anquetilistes." "Poulidorisme" embodied the pastoral romantic spirit, "Anquetilisme," cosmopolitan rationality. Together they provided the yin and yang of sport and of society in general.

But if he forged his reputation as Anquetil's rival, it was Eddy Merckx who offered Poulidor his renaissance. Like Anquetil, Merckx's strength was supreme. And like Anquetil, Merckx brought out the best in Poulidor. In 1969, the first year of Merckx's reign, Poulidor finished an honorable

third, a feat he repeated in 1972, the year of Merckx's fourth victory. And in 1974, Merckx's fifth victory, Poulidor astounded everyone by being the closest rival.

"In 1964 I was Anquetil's biggest threat, and in 1974 I was Merckx's main rival," Poulidor says as he recalls his two near-miss Tour victories. Certainly Merckx was not one to forget Poulidor's memorable stage win in that same year. After Poulidor powered away in the Pyrenees to win the stage to Saint-Lary-Soulan, Merckx admitted with rare admiration, "Let me tell you something. In the Pyrenees he [Poulidor] taught us all a lesson."

Although Poulidor never rode as brilliantly as these superrivals, he certainly rode longer. In 1976, after fifteen years of professional cycling, Poulidor again pulled out a vintage performance in the Tour by finishing third.

But then the Tour always brought out Poulidor's best. Even if the best was never quite good enough.

EDDY MERCKX: THE MAN WHO ATE MEN

EDDY ARRIVES. MERCKX CRUISES INTO PARIS'S VINCENNES VÉLODROME ON THE WAY TO HIS FIRST TOUR TITLE IN 1969. IT WOULD NOT BE HIS LAST.

Because of his insatiable appetite for devouring the competition, they called him "the Cannibal." Bicycle racing had never before seen the likes of Eddy Merckx, and it certainly hasn't seen the likes of him since. His reign was arguably the greatest the sport had ever seen, and as far as champions are concerned, Merckx was a dictator. He was so focused on winning that the smallest defeat in the most insignificant of races could set him off for days.

Marc Jeaniau, one of Merckx's biographers, tells how at the end of one of his best seasons, Merckx lost the Putte-Kappelle race, Belgium's season-closing kermesse race, a simple criterium. Mortified, he fell into a depression for several days. Suddenly his victories in Milan–San Remo, Paris-Roubaix, and the Tour de France meant nothing. He had lost Putte-Kappelle! But then for Merckx, winning always remained a question of honor. Losing brought nothing but shame.

For Merckx, the only antidepressant was victory, and throughout his thirteen-year professional career he reveled in this remedy 525 times. Not bad for a kid who delivered milk so that he could buy his first bicycle.

He etched his name in the annals of virtually every major race: three World Championships, five Tours de France, five Tours of Italy, seven Milan–San Remos, three Paris-Roubaix, three Paris-Nices, and the World Hour Record. And yes, the list does go on. About the only major race he did not win was Paris-Tours. That race is known as the "sprinter's classic," and there are few opportunities for strong men like Merckx to flex their muscles and break away.

When Merckx first rode the Tour de France in 1969, the old guard knew their days were numbered. "I've never felt so old," uttered Raymond Poulidor, at the mercy of Merckx. For Roger Pingeon, Merckx was quite simply "above the laws of nature." He rode so effortlessly in his Tour debut that often he never gave the impression of attacking; the competition simply withered.

Race tactics seemed to be his only weakness. But with his supreme strength, who needed to think? During his first victory in the great Belgian classic, the Tour of Flanders—the virtual world championship for Flemish cycling—Merckx showed what he thought of tactics. Breaking away seventy kilometers from the finish, Merckx threw caution to the wind—and to the rain that blanketed the day. Even his team director, Guillaume Driessens, who had directed legends like Fausto Coppi and Rik Van Looy, saw the move as frivolous. Pulling alongside Merckx, he pleaded, "This is pure folly! I beg you to stop. You'll never make it to the end." Merckx promptly responded, "Go screw yourself," then proceeded to show Driessens what he thought of such conventional wisdom. He powered on alone to win by over five minutes. And Driessens didn't last long as his director.

Each time Merckx started the Tour over the next five years, his competition simply had to settle for the crumbs of his glory. Journalists were forced to describe the success of others in relation to the "Merckx shadow." Only Luis Ocana managed to destabilize Merckx during his reign, but the cometlike career of the Spaniard never provided any lasting threat. After taking the lead from Merckx in the 1971 Tour, he crashed and abandoned. The one year that Ocana did win was the one year Merckx opted not to compete in the three-week race.

Merckx did have a few setbacks, like the tragic accident on the Bois vélodrome in 1969, when the lights on the track suddenly went out while he was motorpacing behind his trainer. The crash cost the motorcycle driver his life, and Merckx seriously injured his back. After that crash the Belgian always complained that he never climbed the same. His opponents, however, only tremble to think how many more races he might have won without the ensuing back ailments from that fateful crash.

When Tour defeat finally did hit in 1975, it was due as much to Merckx's own weakness as it was to the strength of the new champion, Bernard Thévenet. Although he was still suffering from the bruises received when a spectator punched him on the Puy-de-Dôme climb several days earlier, Merckx refused to lay low to better recuperate. With the yellow jersey on his shoulders, common sense would be to ride defensively. Instead, he attacked early on stage fifteen. For a while he even looked to be on his way to a record sixth victory. Suddenly, though, on the final climb to Pra-Loup, Merckx came up empty. As he sputtered toward the finish, Thevenet passed him, eventually taking the yellow jersey.

Tour defeat marked the beginning of the end for Merckx. He continued to accumulate victories of varying significance for several years. And in 1978, when he realized that even the smallest victory was out of reach, he called a press conference and announced his retirement. For the Cannibal, cycling was only about winning.

MERCKX CHASES THÉVENET ALONE ON THE GALIBIER.

MERCKX TAKES A VICTORY LAP AFTER HIS FIRST TOUR WIN IN 1969.

MERCKX MAKES IT FOUR. GIMONDI (LEFT) WAS PLENTY
HAPPY TO FINISH SECOND. THE ITALIAN WAS JUST ONE OF
MANY RIDERS WHO WOULD HAVE HAD A LONGER LIST OF
VICTORIES IF NOT FOR THE BELGIAN.

MERCKX CHALKS UP HIS FOURTH VICTORY
IN 1972, DESPITE THE TIRELESS POULIDOR.

1969–1975:
THE MERCKX YEARS

MERCKX SOLOING TO HIS FIRST TOUR TRIUMPH IN 1969.

1969: *AN ICON IS BORN* Eddy Merckx arrived at the 1969 Tour riding a bicycle named after him, an honor usually bestowed on aging superstars. But Merckx was no ordinary rider. He'd already taken the top prize in dozens of important races, including Paris-Roubaix and Milan–San Remo, and he had even earned his first World Championship title.

After a positive drug test in the Tour of Italy—a charge he still flatly denies—Merckx came to the 1969 Tour looking for revenge. And it didn't take him long to get it.

Once the race began, Merckx won two of the first six stages and bolted into the lead. On the first mountain stage over the Ballon d'Alsace in eastern France, he dropped two of his toughest challengers, Italian rider Felice Gimondi and France's Raymond Poulidor. The 1967 Tour winner, French rider Roger Pingeon, gave the most determined fight. He won the Alpine stage to Chamonix and stayed with Merckx longer than any other cyclist.

In fact, thanks to Merckx's reputation, Pingeon's perseverance won him as much respect as his 1967 Tour victory. Before the end of the race, though, Merckx won three time trials and three

more stages, and he had a seventeen-minute lead over Pingeon when the race returned to Paris.

Merckx rode so effortlessly in his Tour debut that he often literally rode away from the field without trying. On one occasion, over the Tourmalet pass in the Pyrenees, Merckx thought he was simply pacing the lead group. "But suddenly, when I looked around, no one was left," he recalls. Not one to wait around, Merckx continued his effort over the Aubisque pass. Nearly one hundred kilometers later he rolled toward the stage finish in Mourenx with his nearest chasers nearly eight minutes behind.

In addition to his six stage wins, Merckx won every category in the 1969 Tour, including the white jersey, distinguishing the best young rider, and the green points jersey. But through most of the race he wore the most prestigious jersey, the yellow jersey.

Reverent Italians labeled his aggressive style of racing "Merckxissimo," and for the French, 1969 was the dawning of "Merckxisme." But a relatively unknown French rider, Christian Raymond, coined the phrase that would endure. During the race, Raymond was so impressed with Merckx's ability to consume the pack that he labeled him "the Cannibal."

1970: *CONFIRMATION OF THE CANNIBAL* For many, the 1970 Tour was little more than a race for second place. Merckx had seized the power from the older generation of riders the preceding year, and the younger generation still lacked the experience to challenge him. The promising French neoprofessional Bernard Thévenet attracted much attention by winning an impressive mountain stage in the Pyrenees, but the overall classification was still well out of his reach.

The dearth of competition didn't cause the insatiable champion to hold back. But then, Merckx never knew how to bite the bit. He matched his 1969 record, again scoring six stage wins. Merckx, however, proved himself mortal on the brutal climb to the summit of Mont Ventoux. He won the stage, but afterward he collapsed in the middle of an interview and required an oxygen mask to recover.

He wasn't able to dominate the Pyrenees that year, but by the final time trial, Merckx had recuperated and once again took the overall honors. When he rode to the finish line in Paris, he was twelve minutes and forty-one seconds ahead of the competition.

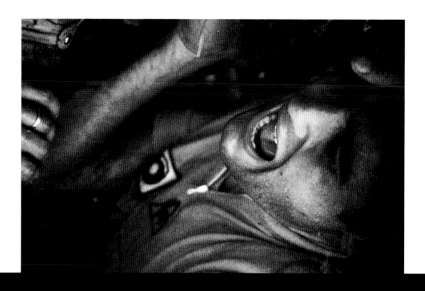

1971: OCANA'S SURPRISE The start of the 1971 Tour seemed to promise even less suspense. As usual, Merckx dominated his competition throughout the classics. And after victories in traditional Tour warm-up races like the Midi-Libre and the Dauphiné-Libéré, he appeared to be well on his way to matching Jacques Anquetil's record of five Tour wins.

As expected, Merckx took the lead immediately. His powerful Molteni team won the team time trial, and Merckx won the second stage. But the next generation of young riders—filled with talents like Bernard Thévenet and Luis Ocana—kept the pressure on with constant attacks. On the first climbing stage to the top of the Puy de Dôme, Merckx couldn't defend himself from Ocana's furious efforts to break away. "What do you expect?" defended the Belgian. "I cracked. I'm only human." Ocana, however, was never one to gloat, and he was playing it cautiously: "With this devil Merckx, anything is possible," is all he would say.

In the Alps, Merckx again could only look on as Ocana soared to victory on the stage from Grenoble to Orcières-Merlette. At the finish, Ocana grabbed a nine-minute advantage. The yellow jersey was now his. Merckx immediately responded with a surprise attack at the start of the next stage. At the finish in Marseille, nearly 250 kilometers later, Merckx had recouped more than two minutes from the Spaniard. But Ocana still had a solid hold on the jersey.

Then disaster struck. In the Pyrenees, on the stage from Revel to Luchon, storms transformed the race into a nightmare. Merckx attacked relentlessly—without success. Ocana, never a good rain rider, was glued to Merckx's wheel. But as the two descended the Col de Mente, the young Spanish star missed a turn and crashed into a ravine. Suddenly, his Tour was over.

The event shook Merckx, even though Ocana wasn't seriously injured. Merckx refused to wear the yellow jersey the next day. He even considered abandoning, because he knew Ocana could have won the race if it weren't for the accident. After much encouragement from his teammates, though, he continued, won the final time trial, and took his third consecutive Tour.

1972: THE CANNIBAL MAINTAINS HIS APPETITE Merckx, now a three-time defending champion, appeared haunted at the 1972 Tour. Still suffering from the memory of the previous year's crash that eliminated Ocana, he lacked his characteristic confidence.

Almost more than victory itself, Merckx set out to show he still had the best lungs and legs of any Tour rider. Ocana was again present but not at his best. French riders Bernard Thévenet and Cyrille Guimard and Belgian rider Lucien Van Impe all won impressive stages.

Merckx, however, showed that he was again his old self by winning six stages and generally dominating the race. He won the prologue, both time trials, and two mountain stages in both the Pyrenees and the Alps. When he rode into Paris, he led by ten minutes. Clearly, he had proved his point.

MERCKX (CENTER) WITH
ZOETEMELK (LEFT) AND
VAN IMPE (RIGHT), TWO
OF HIS MOST FAITHFUL
FOLLOWERS.

1973: OCANA TAKES THE TOUR

After winning three classics—Milan–San Remo, Liège-Bastogne-Liège, and Flèche Wallonne—along with the Tour of Spain and the Tour of Italy, Merckx graciously opted to sit out the 1973 Tour. It was time to rest and to give others a chance. Eddy's absence gave Luis Ocana an opportunity for a consolation victory after the tragedy that had cost him the Tour two years earlier.

With a symbolic start in Holland, Dutch rider Joop Zoetemelk showed that he felt comfortable on his home turf. From the start of the race he took the lead and donned the yellow jersey. French riders Raymond Poulidor and Bernard Thévenet, however, applied constant pressure—but nothing compared to Ocana.

Once in the mountains, Ocana's fetish terrain, he humiliated his rivals. On the second and hardest Alpine stage, Ocana rode away from all his challengers. He left his closest rivals seven minutes behind on the legendary Izoard and Galibier passes.

Then he went on to pick up the first time-trial stage and a mountain stage in the Pyrenees. And just for safekeeping, Ocana beat Thévenet by over twelve minutes on the stage to Puy de Dôme. And when the race finally returned to Paris, Ocana remained fifteen minutes ahead of his nearest competitor.

1974: MERCKX'S TRIUMPHANT RETURN

Merckx returned to the Tour in 1974, only to face increasingly confident challengers. To his advantage, the defending champion, Spanish rider Luis Ocana, didn't enter the race because of health problems.

Merckx started strong by winning the prologue, but his first stage victory didn't come until stage six. He then struggled through the mountains and was even surpassed by the aging Raymond Poulidor. On the Alpine stage from Aspro Gaillard

"THE CANNIBAL" GRIMACES THROUGH HIS LAST PEDAL STROKES IN THE YELLOW JERSEY AFTER HE IS DROPPED BY BERNARD THÉVENET ON THE CLIMB UP COL D'ALLOS IN THE 1975 TOUR.

to Aix-les-Bains, Merckx was one minute and forty-five seconds behind Poulidor at one point. A devilish descender, Merckx managed to recoup his deficit in one of the greatest chases in Tour history: at least one follow vehicle, that of team director Giancarlo Ferretti, ended up in a ditch trying to keep up with the Cannibal. Merckx continued his hot pursuit, caught up with Poulidor, and then beat the veteran to the finish line.

From there on out, Merckx paced himself sufficiently to ensure a win. It may not have been his most impressive victory, but it was his fifth, thus tying him with the French record holder, Jacques Anquetil.

1975: THE DEMISE OF EDDY MERCKX Five-time-defending-champion Eddy Merckx arrived at the 1975 Tour in the midst of one of his best seasons. He had just won Milan–San Remo, the Tour of Flanders, and Liège-Bastogne-Liège, and he was wearing the World Champion's rainbow jersey.

As usual, Merckx donned the yellow jersey the opening week. He snared the first time trial and entered the mountains more than two minutes ahead of the competition. But the mountains proved even more troublesome than they had a year earlier. France's climbing specialist Bernard Thévenet and Dutch rider Joop Zoetemelk attacked constantly and nearly cracked Merckx.

In the Alps, Merckx bluffed supremely. Just when his opponents thought he was on the verge of tiring, he attacked. Tour vehicles couldn't keep up, and a few ended up in the ravines when they tried following his harrowing descents.

On stage fifteen, from Nice to Pra-Loup, Merckx appeared primed for his sixth Tour title. With just six kilometers remaining, he was ahead by one minute. But Thévenet returned at a pace that humbled Merckx. Four kilometers from the summit, the Cannibal cracked and staggered to the finish. Merckx still held the yellow jersey, but Thévenet

won the next stage to Serre Chevalier, forcing Merckx to relinquish the lead.

Faced with defeat, Merckx spoke with humility: "I tried everything and it didn't work. Miracles don't exist in sports. It's always the strongest who wins. And the strongest is Thévenet."

MOSER MAKES A BRIEF VISIT Italian champion Francesco Moser never much liked the Tour de France. He only raced it one year. But in 1975 he left his mark. Grabbing the yellow jersey during the opening stage in Charleroi, Belgium, the twenty-four-year-old Italian challenged Merckx's superiority in front of the Cannibal's native fans. Although he eventually finished a promising seventh and won two stages as well as the best-young-rider award, Moser apparently didn't like what he saw. Or at least he felt the climb to the top remained out of reach. He never again entered the Tour.

BERNARD HINAULT (FAR RIGHT) SHIFTS INTO OVER-DRIVE DURING A STAGE SPRINT IN THE 1981 TOUR.

BERNARD HINAULT: THEY DIDN'T CALL HIM "THE BADGER" FOR NOTHING

AFTER CRASHING IN THE FINAL KILOMETER OF STAGE FOURTEEN INTO SAINT ETIENNE IN 1985, A FRACTURED NOSE COMPROMISED HINAULT'S CHANCES FOR A FIFTH TOUR WIN.

HINAULT GRUNTS THROUGH HIS SEVENTY-SIXTH AND LAST DAY IN THE YELLOW JERSEY. AND HE DOESN'T LOOK MUCH WORSE FOR WEAR.

Great champions have a way of making their presences known immediately. And like Jacques Anquetil and Eddy Merckx before him, France's Bernard Hinault did so by winning the first Tour de France he ever contested. So respected was he among his peers that the young star even led a riders' strike protesting long transfers.

For many, Hinault was the last of the "patrons," that rare breed of champion whose superior physical strength is matched by their individual character. These unique riders acted as senior statesmen both on and off the bike.

Henri Pélissier was one of these patrons. So were greats like Louison Bobet, Jacques Anquetil, and Eddy Merckx. Since Hinault, the general level of cycling has increased so much that the difference between team leader and team worker has diminished. Many riders since have possessed the physical strength, and others have had the charisma. But not one has managed to have both.

As the last "boss" of the peloton, Hinault was a frank and sometimes blunt spokesman for the sport. About the only thing worse than "the Badger's" bark was his bite; Hinault could back up his words with his legs and lungs.

Hinault possessed a hearty dose of "nice-guys-finish-last" mentality. Once a race started, only winning counted. He first captured the respect of his public in the 1977 Dauphiné-Libéré when, after crashing on the descent of the Col de Porte, he climbed out of the ravine, remounted his bike, and rode to victory on the leg-breaking slopes of Grenoble's Bastille climb. It was a symbolic victory he repeated little more than a year later by winning his first Tour de France.

Like the first Tour victory of Eddy Merckx, that of Bernard Hinault served as a clear signal to the old guard—Raymond Poulidor, Bernard Thévenet, and Lucien Van Impe—that their days were numbered. Of the veterans, only Holland's Joop Zoetemelk managed to eke out a Tour victory during the Hinault reign. But then Zoetemelk's victory was due in part to the fact that the Frenchman dropped out midway because of knee problems. His delicate knee would also open the door to youngster Laurent Fignon in 1983, when Hinault was forced to forfeit after another operation. Fignon again took advantage of Hinault's injury in the 1984 Tour, when he outdistanced the recovering Hinault by ten minutes.

But in the 1985 Tour, Hinault returned in full possession of his much-feared strength. Only his teammate, the young American Greg LeMond, equaled him physically. But the amiable neophyte was no match for Hinault psychologically, and in a complicated affair of team tactics, Hinault assured his fifth Tour de France victory—even though it cost him LeMond's friendship.

Hinault was also the last complete champion, one capable of winning the spring classics, the Tour of Italy, the Tour of Spain, and the Tour de France, as well as the World Championship. Riders today tend to specialize, preferring to concentrate on specific goals.

Unlike other great champions, Bernard Hinault also knew how to retire in style. Fausto Coppi, Jacques Anquetil, and Eddy Merckx all rode past their primes. Bernard Hinault, however, announced years in advance that he would retire at the age of thirty-two. And after wearing the yellow jersey for a spell in the 1986 Tour and winning the Coors Classic that same year, Hinault kept his word.

1978–1985: THE HINAULT YEARS

IT MAY BE VICTORY BY DEFAULT, BUT HOLLAND'S JOOP ZOETEMELK IS HAPPY TO TAKE A TOUR TITLE ANY WAY HE CAN.

1978: HINAULT SAVES THE DAY In 1978 bicycle racing was in search of a new hero. After drug scandals tainted the 1977 Tour, defending champion Bernard Thévenet spent much of the winter hospitalized after his abuse of cortisone had nearly rotted his liver. Once again, drugs, sport's most persistent parasite, had made their mark.

But bicycle racing's ability to survive is linked to its ability to constantly produce new champions, new heroes who offer new reasons to cheer. In 1978 Hinault instantly became that new hero.

After winning the French championship, Hinault had no secrets; he wanted to follow in the footsteps of Fausto Coppi, Hugo Koblet, Jacques Anquetil, and Eddy Merckx by winning his Tour de France debut. Hinault faced steady competition from Joop Zoetemelk, a superior climber and consistent pretender to the Tour title. The Dutch veteran won the telling Puy-de-Dôme stage, but Zoetemelk lacked the initiative necessary to pad his lead.

Hinault, however, never lacked in the initiative department. And when it came to the time trials, Zoetemelk was no match. In the final time trial from Metz to Nancy, Hinault grabbed the yellow jersey and coasted into Paris three minutes and fifty-six seconds in the lead.

STRIKES AND SCANDAL The Tour de France is renowned as one of the world's toughest physical endurance tests, but in 1978 riders felt the race was made unreasonably difficult with exceedingly long transfers. When the pack reached the twelfth stage, organizers had a full-fledged revolt on their hands. On the early-morning stretch between Tarbes and Valence, the racers showed their anger by ambling over the first 157 kilometers at a mere twenty kilometers an hour. They covered the last kilometer on foot.

With the hard-nosed stoicism inherent in Tour de France directors, Jacques Goddet showed little sympathy. "It's necessary to keep an inhuman side to the Tour. Excess is necessary," he insisted.

But such excesses encourage, in part, the use of performance-enhancing drugs. And even after

Bernard Thévenet's eye-opening confession during the previous winter (see page 145), many cyclists remained deaf to warnings about drugs.

Take Belgian Michael Pollentier, for example. During the Alpe d'Huez stage, Pollentier attacked ferociously and won both the stage and the yellow jersey. Afterward, he was supposed to immediately go to the drug-testing center. Instead, he went to his hotel room, where he rigged a contraption to his arm that carried a fake urine sample. He put a long-sleeved jersey on to cover the device, but when it malfunctioned during the test, Pollentier nervously started flagging his arm. Uncovered, Pollentier was immediately thanked for his creativity, dismissed from the Tour, and suspended for two months.

1979: HINAULT DITTO The 1979 route was one of the most challenging in years, with four time trials and eight mountain stages. In fact, the race started in the Pyrenees and made its way up the coast and across northern France and into Belgium before dropping down to the Alps and finally winding back to Paris. Frenchman Bernard Hinault, never one to lack motivation, geared up to defend his title.

Hinault attacked from the start, and he won two out of three mountain stages in the Pyrenees. On the cobbled roads between Amiens and Roubaix during stage nine, though, he flatted twice. Despite a harried chase by Hinault, Holland's Joop Zoetemelk stole the jersey with a two-minute lead. Still, Hinault had stolen the show. France's legendary cyclist Jacques Anquetil said, "Hinault certainly won the Tour today. Anyone else would have lost fifteen minutes."

During the second mountain time trial, Hinault overtook Zoetemelk, and once again the Frenchman donned the yellow jersey. Hinault continued his rampage and took the final time trial to Dijon. By the time he reached the finish line in Paris, he was over three minutes ahead of Zoetemelk.

HINAULT'S SECRET WEAPON—AERODYNAMICS EQUALS STRENGTH In the history of team time-trialing, the Dutch Ti-Raleigh team is recognized as one of the best. Its riders worked together with militarylike efficiency. Throughout the late 1970s and early 1980s, they repeatedly showed that they were the world's strongest team. During the 1979 Tour, many expected the Dutch team to grab an early advantage. However, Hinault's team had a secret weapon. They rode a new breed of aerodynamic bicycles that enabled them to ride faster and secure Hinault's Tour win.

1980: ZOETEMELK'S GIFT With two Tour de France victories already tied down, Hinault was now a certified superstar. But the 1980 race would prove to be a stumbling block.

He again jumped off to a lightning start, winning the prologue, not to mention stages four and five. Mother Nature, however, was clearly not smiling on Hinault. A combination of brutally long stages and driving rains chilled the peloton. Hinault was among some fifty riders suffering from tendonitis.

His team director, Cyrille Guimard, had reason to expect the worst. He remembered all too well how tendonitis had prematurely ended his own career. Hinault hobbled through the first twelve stages but was forced to abandon just as the race entered the Pyrenees.

Long-time challenger Joop Zoetemelk inherited the yellow jersey. Few would deny the Dutchman this unexpected gift. After all, in the 1970s he had finished second five times. Although he faltered in the Alps, his powerful Ti-Raleigh team helped him return to Paris as the winner.

THE HONOR OF THE YELLOW JERSEY Over the years, the yellow jersey has taken on a magical aura. Sometimes referred to as "the golden fleece," it has been known to transform the performance of whoever wears it. Wearing it for only a stage constitutes a career highlight. The jersey commands such reverence that cyclists often refuse to wear it for a day if the former wearer had lost it through misfortune.

Such was the case in 1971, when Belgian rider Eddy Merckx refused to don the jersey after Spanish rider Luis Ocana fell during the descent

of Col de Mente. In 1980, Zoetemelk also waited a day to put on the jersey when tendonitis forced Hinault to abandon.

1981: HINAULT'S REVENGE With the hunger of a neo-professional, Hinault returned to win in 1981. After tendonitis had forced him out of the race only twelve months earlier, he had to establish his presence early on. Adding to the pressure was the rainbow-striped world champion's jersey on his shoulders.

To ensure that he would be fresh for the race, Hinault skipped the Tour of Italy. It proved to be a wise move: Hinault dominated the Tour de France from start to finish. Starting with his patented prologue victory, he eventually won every individual time trial. His climbing had improved as well, and he won the coveted stage to Alpe d'Huez. When the race returned to Paris, Hinault was sitting on a huge fourteen-minute cushion in the overall standings.

AUSTRALIAN ARRIVAL The Australians made their Tour debut in 1914, but Tour glory wouldn't come for another fifty years, when Phil Anderson became the first rider from Down Under to wear the yellow jersey. At the finish line of the first stage in the Pyrenees, Anderson came in third, behind Hinault. But the strong performance of his Peugeot team pushed him into the lead. Anderson's term in yellow, however, would be short-lived. The following stage was an individual time trial, and Anderson was no match for Hinault. But then, nobody was that year.

1982: STATE OF GRACE In the reign of every Tour de France legend, there is one year in which he rides in a state of grace. In 1982, Bernard Hinault was clearly blessed with such a year. With unbridled confidence, the already cocky French star stormed into the race.

A Hinault victory in the prologue was now standard fare. During the three-week race, he briefly lost the yellow jersey to Australian Phil Anderson, but most of his opponents appeared content to race for the other prizes.

A CONFIDENT BERNARD HINAULT CROSSES THE FINAL FINISH LINE ON THE CHAMPS-ELYSÉES FOR HIS FIRST TOUR VICTORY IN 1978.

BACK IN ACTION, HINAULT MAKES IT THREE IN 1981. KEEPING HIM COMPANY ON THE FINAL PODIUM ARE (FROM LEFT TO RIGHT) FREDDY MAERTENS, ROBERT ALBAN, HINAULT, LUCIEN VAN IMPE, AND PETER WINNEN.

Irish racer Sean Kelly continued the new English-speaking insurgence by winning the green sprinter's jersey—his first of four. As a matter of habit, Joop Zoetemelk of the Netherlands took second place. But really there was little suspense.

Ironically, Hinault's performance was less spectacular than in previous years. He lost the first time trial and did not win a mountain stage. But he rode with such confidence and consistency that he was never seriously challenged.

1983–84: HINAULT'S HIBERNATION

For much of his career, it seemed, Bernard Hinault's worst enemy was himself—or at least his knees. Tendonitis in his knee forced him to abandon with the yellow jersey on his shoulders in 1980, and similar knee injuries kept him out of the 1983 Tour.

For veterans like Joop Zoetemelk of the Netherlands and Belgium's Lucien Van Impe, Hinault's absence offered a rare opportunity. But instead it was Hinault's apprentice—the up-and-coming Laurent Fignon—who captured the headlines. A war of succession saw the jersey switch shoulders frequently. But no one could take control. Unheralded Frenchman Pascal Simon jumped into the lead in the Pyrenees but then promptly proceeded to break his shoulder on the next stage.

The following week the Tour was transformed into a virtual funeral march. Simon had no chance of keeping the lead with only one good shoulder, but no rider wanted to attack the yellow jersey when he was down.

When Simon could no longer follow the leaders, Fignon took over. He had ridden impressively in the Tour of Spain, serving as one of Hinault's key workers. Now he was making an equally impressive Tour debut.

Transformed with the "golden fleece" on his shoulders, Fignon rode consistently in the Alps and won the final time trial to Dijon. At the age of twenty-two, he became one of the youngest riders to take the top prize since Henri Cornet did it at the age of twenty in 1904.

1984: DUBIOUS RETURN

The big news in France was that Bernard Hinault was back. But now, instead of malleable riders like Joop Zoetemelk as challengers, he had to deal with a feisty Laurent Fignon. Since Fignon was once Hinault's disciple on the Renault team, he knew what made the Badger snap—and crack.

During the winter, Hinault had joined the new La Vie Claire team, leaving Fignon to lead the legendary Renault squad alone. One thing was certain: the duel between them promised to hold France spellbound. And it did.

As usual, Hinault took the lead from the outset by winning the prologue. But Fignon tortured Hinault in the mountains. On the crucial stage from Grenoble to Alpe d'Huez, Fignon toyed with Hinault as the impatient veteran attacked repeatedly on the minor climbs leading up to the finish. Then on the final climb up the Alpe d'Huez, Fignon floored his one-time teacher.

Shouldering the yellow jersey, Fignon even had the supreme pleasure of beating Hinault at his own game: winning the final time trial in Beaujolais.

BONJOUR TO THE AMERICANS

For the first time in the history of the sport, the Tour de France took on a distinctly American flavor in 1984.

North Americans were particularly interested in a certain Greg LeMond, who took third in the race. The same year, U.S. cyclist Marianne Martin won the inaugural Tour for women.

And South Americans put their stamp on the 1984 Tour when the Colombians fielded a team for the second consecutive year. After having attacked incessantly in the Pyrenees the year before, Luis Herrera brought his country fame in 1984 by winning the legendary stage to Alpe d'Huez.

1985: THE BADGER IS BACK

In the continuing saga of damaged tendons, it was now Laurent Fignon's turn to sit out, as the two-time defending champion suffered a bad case of the achilles tendonitis blues.

Hinault was clearly back in force and was eyeing his fifth Tour title, a feat that would put him in the record books along with Jacques Anquetil and Eddy Merckx. Ironically, his toughest competition came from another of his disciples, American Greg LeMond. Hinault thought he had covered his bases by hiring LeMond on the La Vie Claire team.

But when the French star crashed in the final kilometer of stage fourteen, LeMond demonstrated that he was in a position to take over. Hinault, however, was already in the yellow jersey, thus cornering LeMond into a subordinate support role. On stage seventeen, up the Luz Ardiden climb in the Pyrenees, LeMond covered a breakaway with Irish rider Stephen Roche and dropped Hinault. But the American was soon reminded that he had been hired to work for Hinault, not to defeat him. And instead of going on the attack, he had to bite the bit.

At the finish, LeMond was in tears. Hinault, knowing that LeMond's sacrifice would assure his fifth Tour win, pledged to return the favor the following year. But when the following year came, Hinault was once again the defending champion, and he did not appear to be in the mood to be handing out any favors.

GREG LEMOND LEADS A YOUNG MIGUEL INDURIAN IN THE FINAL
KILOMETR OF THE LUZ-ARDIDEN CLIMB IN THE 1990 TOUR.

GREG LEMOND:
RACING BIKES HIS WAY

CANADIAN STEVE BAUER, A FRIEND OF LEMOND'S, WORE THE YELLOW JERSEY IN 1988 AND 1990, THUS DOING HIS SHARE TO CONFIRM THE STRONG ANGLOPHONE INFLUENCE IN EUROPEAN RACING IN THE 1980s AND '90s.

Greg LeMond tends to get taken for granted these days. Twenty years after he first moved to Europe and turned professional, the accomplishments of the American pioneer cyclist are too easily overlooked. And the dismal final years of his career provide an unfitting ending to his achievements. But then maybe his long-time rival Laurent Fignon summed it up best at the end of his own career when he said, "It's not how you finish that matters. It's what you did when you were at the top that counts."

Since LeMond first forged his way through the French professional system and rose to the summit of the sport in the early 1980s, waves of others have mimicked his efforts. Each year another handful of young American cyclists comes to Europe, signs up with an amateur club, and chases their cycling dream. It's always the same dream— turn professional and someday ride in the Tour de France. Numerous American-owned professional teams also have spent their seasons in Europe.

With all the followers, what set LeMond apart gets muddled, and his accomplishments get overshadowed. But look at the record books— a win list that included three Tours de France and two World Championships.

When Greg LeMond first came to Europe as a fresh-faced nineteen-year-old, he was overwhelmed by the retrograde old-boy style that was the world of professional cycling. In the States, cycling was a sport for the affluent, but on the continent it still labored in its reputation as a poor man's sport.

LeMond did make a few faux pas. Sneaking an occasional ice cream after dinner didn't win him many points, and neither did his golf game. If, like most teenagers, he still had a certain naïveté, he was certainly ill-equipped for the manipulative methods of Cyrille Guimard, his first coach on the Renault team. When Guimard ridiculed him for starting one season overweight, LeMond felt as

ANDY HAMPSTEN, A LEMOND DISCIPLE, CLIMBING THE ALPE D'HUEZ IN 1990. HE WOULD RETURN TO WIN THE MYTHIC MOUNTAIN STAGE IN 1992.

though his mentor had turned on him. He did not yet understand that such mind games were standard fare for this Machiavelli-style director.

And in 1986, he was unprepared for the relentless mind games inflicted upon him by his other key mentor, Bernard Hinault. After LeMond supported Hinault in 1985, the five-time Tour winner promised to ride for l'américain the following year. But when Tour time came, and Hinault saw that he could be the first six-time winner, his promise turned transparent.

But on both occasions LeMond bridled his wide-eyed dismay with a hearty dose of determination. And both times he came out a winner. He responded to Guimard by losing the weight and winning races, like the 1983 World Championship. And he eventually wore down Hinault to win the 1986 Tour.

Really, revolutionary is the best word to describe Greg LeMond. Throughout his fifteen-year professional career, the American star never ceased to transform the traditional, closed world of European bicycle racing. Almost single-handedly he led the cause of internationalization in the sport, and English-speaking fans from around the world lived vicariously through his exploits—and his tragedy.

With his first victories, he demanded that he receive a salary similar to professional athletes in his own country. LeMond grew up in the land of the free-agent athlete don't forget. He knew what he was worth and he would not accept the notion that cycling was still a working-class sport. He got what he asked for, becoming the first million-dollar cyclist. And as a result, the average salary of lesser riders also increased.

In addition to money, he always maintained an eye for technological advances that could improve his performance. Thus, few were surprised when he began time trialing with triathlon-style handlebars in the 1989 Tour de France. Moreover, his carefree lifestyle also provided lessons, and he showed that, despite the demands of cycling, athletes did not have to live like monks. They could enjoy frivolities like ice cream sundaes and golf. Previously riders who displayed such "unprofessional behavior" flirted with a breach of contract.

LeMond could do all these things and get away with them because he did something else extremely well: win bicycle races. Already in his first year as a professional he showed enormous potential, and when he became world champion at the age of twenty-two, it became clear that the young American represented one of the greatest talents of his generation.

He confirmed all the expectations placed on him by defeating Bernard Hinault in the 1986 Tour de France, despite the Frenchman's unrelenting war of nerves. Hinault claimed he only wanted to prepare the rising star for what would face him once his mentor retired. Although Hinault's true motives were probably more self-centered, LeMond likely benefited from the apprenticeship.

Only months later, LeMond was lying in a hospital bed, the victim of a hunting accident. His return to competition was long and slow, and his return to victory even slower.

In July of 1989, however, LeMond proved that he possessed the unrelenting drive inherent in all great champions with his against-all-odds comeback win in the Tour de France. For much of the race Laurent Fignon, another Guimard/Hinault—schooled star, controlled the race. But LeMond refused to relinquish, despite the odds. And when he charged down the Champs-Elysées eight seconds in front of his rival, LeMond showed himself to be one of the greatest champions in the history of the sport.

One year later, he defended his Tour title to complete a memorable triple. Certainly the third Tour win was not his most glorious. He struggled in the early season, and pictures show that he was not at his

SOUTH AMERICANS ALSO MADE THEIR MARK IN THE TOUR. FABIO PARRA (LEFT) AND LOUIS "LUCHO" HERRERA (RIGHT) REPRESENTED THE CREAM OF COLOMBIAN CYCLING. PARRA FINISHED THIRD IN 1988, AND HERRERA TWICE WON THE BEST CLIMBER AWARD.

ideal weight during the race. He nearly saw the race slip away from him when the unheralded Italian rider Claudio Chiappucci jumped into a surprise early break and grabbed the yellow jersey.

"Greg was so nervous throughout much of the race," remembered his Z team captain, Gilbert Duclos-Lassalle. "Most of the race I spent simply trying to calm him down, to assure him that Chiappucci would eventually fold."

But in the end, LeMond was a smart tactician as well as one of the most consistent riders of his generation. When LeMond was on, the much-feared

jour sans, or "off day," simply did not exist. On the final time trial around the Lac de Vassivière, Chiappucci did fold, and LeMond finally grabbed the yellow jersey for good.

At the start of the 1991 Tour, he looked set to strike again. On the attack early in the race, LeMond quickly put many of his rivals on the defensive. He was riding so confidently that he even refused to take over the yellow jersey the day after Danish rider Rolf Sörenson lost it in a crash.

But once the race entered the Pyrenees, LeMond slowly folded and a new line of stars—Miguel

Indurain and Gianni Bugno—took over. Still, LeMond finished a respectable seventh, and he even managed to pay homage to the Tour by leading a symbolic charge around the Champs-Elysées on the final stage.

Honor in the Tour, however, became increasingly evasive. Although he would start each season with the enthusiasm of a newcomer, LeMond never managed to finish another Tour.

GREG LEMOND WARMS UP FOR THE 1994 PROLOGUE. IT WOULD BE HIS LAST.

1986–1990:THE LEMOND YEARS — AMERICAN LEADS FOREIGN INFLUENCE IN FRENCH RACE

EVEN IF THEY RODE FOR OPPOSING TEAMS, GREG LEMOND KNEW THAT ROBERT MILLAR WAS A GOOD WHEEL TO FOLLOW IN THE MOUNTAINS.

THE GREEN SPRINTER'S JERSEY PROVED TO BE A GOOD COLOR FOR IRISHMAN SEAN KELLY. HE WON IT FOUR TIMES.

The convergence of numerous international riders onto the European bike-racing scene that characterized the 1980s changed the face of racing at all levels, including the Tour de France. The big players no longer came exclusively from stronghold countries like Italy, Belgium, or France, but also from smaller countries such as Ireland and Denmark, or from as far away as Russia. In fact, the French are still looking for a successor to Bernard Hinault, because, unlikely as it may seem, no Frenchman has won the great French race since Hinault's last victory in 1985.

Ironically, nearly all the great champions of the LeMond era saw their careers plagued with injuries. Question marks and "what ifs" remain with all of them. What if Laurent Fignon hadn't missed the best of the 1985 season with achilles tendonitis. What if Stephen Roche hadn't suffered constantly from knee problems. And of course, what if Greg LeMond had never been accidentally shot.

1986: LEMOND, NO THANKS TO HINAULT. Only twelve
months earlier the 1986 Tour seemed promised to Greg LeMond. After sacrificing his own chances in 1985 to help Hinault win his fifth Tour title, the French star promised to ride for LeMond in 1986. But promises, it is said, are made to be broken. And certainly that is never more the case than when a Tour de France title is on the line.

Yes, Hinault made a promise to LeMond. But then Hinault didn't earn the nickname the Badger for nothing. His mercenary approach to bike racing has fueled more than one discussion around the dinner table or at the bar, not to mention a few heated discussions within the peloton itself. And apparently once Hinault could taste an unprecedented sixth Tour victory, honoring old vows suddenly appeared frivolous. When the 1986 race started, Hinault had clearly changed his tune. Now he said he would work for his American teammate, provided that "Greg shows he is worthy of the yellow jersey."

Who, though, ever really thought that Hinault would give a Tour de France away? Perhaps only LeMond, whose sense of honor came from a world other than the closed circles of European bike racing.

Even before they had arrived at the mountains, Hinault surprised LeMond by going on the attack. Clearly the Frenchman understood that his most serious rival was his own American teammate. By grabbing an early advantage, he could again wedge LeMond into the support role. So, on the stage from Bayonne to Pau, the day before the Tour entered the Pyrenees, Hinault went on the offensive with Spain's Pedro Delgado. LeMond could do nothing but wait . . . and weep. Could his Tour chances already be over?

When Hinault attacked again the following day in the mountains on the stage from Pau to Superbagnères, LeMond again appeared cornered. But over the many years of his career, Hinault had also earned a reputation as a bluffer. And Hinault's bluff was up. The Badger, it seemed, had finally cashed his check.

On the last climb to Superbagnères, the Frenchman faltered. He may have been one of the greatest riders of all time. But on that day, Hinault also proved to be just a regular guy. He too could experience the infamous "bonk," that moment when one's body is depleted of its sugar reserves and simply runs out of fuel.

As Hinault faltered, LeMond returned, and with another teammate, Andy Hampsten, he dropped Hinault. Hampsten, like LeMond one of the fresh Yankee faces in the European peloton, would prove to be LeMond's greatest ally in this telling Tour.

In the Alps, LeMond clearly appeared superior to Hinault. After dropping Hinault again on stage seventeen from Gap to the Col du Granon, LeMond tried on the sacred yellow jersey for the first time in his career. Indeed, he proved he was "worthy."

When Hinault and LeMond finished one-two on the Alpe d'Huez climb the next day, a symbolic

LEMOND STARTS THE FINAL TIME TRIAL IN THE 1989 TOUR. TWENTY-SIX MINUTES AND FIFTY-SEVEN SECONDS LATER, VICTORY WOULD BE HIS.

change of power seemed to be taking place. But the Badger, as stubborn as his nickname implied, held the Tour in suspense by refusing to relinquish. "We'll see on the final time trial who the real winner is," he stated.

Hinault did in fact win that final time trial, a fifty-eight-kilometer grudge match around the not-so-pretty town of Saint-Étienne. But despite crashing in a turn, LeMond only finished twenty-five seconds behind.

Finally he could smile. The Tour was his.

OFF THE TRACK: LEMOND SHOT! In February of 1987, just six months after winning the Tour de France for the first time, American Greg LeMond was nearly killed in a hunting accident in Colorado. It was not known if he would ever be able to compete again. The news was a shock to the cycling world. LeMond was the first American to win the Tour. He represented the increasing internationalization of the sport and had been expected to replace Bernard Hinault as the peloton's new boss. Fate would have it otherwise.

LeMond's recovery was slow. It took him two years to once again become a contender. But once he did, he made it clear that he had not forgotten how to win.

1987: IRISH LUCK ADDS TO AMERICAN MISERY

Greg LeMond couldn't defend his first Tour de France title. Gunshot wounds from a hunting accident in February took care of that. And with Bernard Hinault now retired, the 1987 Tour was an open affair.

Irish hopeful Stephen Roche had matured significantly in the past twelve months, and after winning the Tour of Italy in the spring, he entered the French race with added confidence. But he also had to contend with new rivals such as Spain's Pedro Delgado and Hinault's hand-picked successor, Jean-François Bernard.

After winning the stage-ten time trial, a grueling eighty-seven-and-a-half-kilometer effort from Saumur to Futuroscope, the Irishman made a

good point. Anyone hoping to win the Tour would have to reckon with him. Bernard responded later in the race with an inspired time-trial win up Mont Ventoux. He beat Roche by over two minutes, and at the victory protocol said coyly, "I think yellow becomes me." He was of course speaking of his newly acquired yellow jersey.

But Tour glory for Bernard was short-lived. He flatted and lost the jersey on the following stage, and despite the hype, he never again wore the "becoming" shirt in his country's celebrated race.

Delgado, however, was clearly superior in the Alps, and after an all-or-nothing chase to the mountain-top finish in La Plagne, Roche even needed the help of an oxygen mask to recover. But despite his shortness of breath, Roche cut his losses and on the final time trial took over the yellow jersey for good.

1988: DELGADO: DOPED OR DUPED With Greg LeMond, Stephen Roche, and Laurent Fignon all on the comeback trail, Spain's Pedro Delgado soared to victory in this transitional Tour. But Delgado's Tour win would always be suspect after news broke of a positive drug test midway through the race.

Throughout this mountainous Tour, Delgado was clearly the *crème de la crème*. But when news of his failed drug test after a stage victory in Villard-de-Lans surfaced in Bordeaux, the Tour hobbled back to Paris in humiliation.

In the end Delgado was cleared due to a technicality. The substance in question was banned by the Olympic Committee but was not to be added to the list by the International Cycling Union until the following month. Thus, under a cloud of suspicion, Delgado saved his shirt. In the eyes of many, however, he had lost all honor.

1989: WHO WOULD HAVE BELIEVED? Who would have believed that Greg LeMond would ever again be a Tour contender, let alone a Tour winner? After all, it had been nearly three years since the American won his first Tour in 1986. And, frankly, he had shown little of his old spark. Near-fatal hunting accidents have a way of snuffing out one's genius.

AFTER YEARS OF INJURY, 1987 WINNER STEPHEN ROCHE BID FAREWELL TO PROFESSIONAL CYCLING IN 1993.

AFTER SPENDING HIS BEST YEARS AS AN AMATEUR WITH THE EAST GERMAN NATIONAL TEAM, OLAF LUDWIG FINALLY TURNED PROFESSIONAL IN THE LATE 1980s. AND HE QUICKLY CUT THE MUSTARD, WINNING THE GREEN POINTS JERSEY IN 1990.

Even after LeMond finished second in the final time trial of the Tour of Italy in June, few imagined he could parlay such a performance into overall victory in the Tour de France. But despite his hunting accident, despite three years of poor form and the fact that LeMond was now riding for the insignificant ADR team, he did win the 1989 Tour. And how!

The revived American first gave signs of renewed life when he jumped into the yellow jersey in the opening time trial. Already his comeback seemed complete. But he was not yet ready to start celebrating.

His former teammate Laurent Fignon was making a comeback of his own. He grabbed the splendid shirt on the last stage in the Pyrenees, and the two would play yellow-jersey Ping-Pong for the rest of the race.

LeMond recaptured the lead on the second time trial of the Tour. Fignon tried to isolate the American by complaining that he lacked initiative. Perhaps LeMond was guilty as charged, but he defended himself by saying that he could count on no team support and still did not know where his true capacity lay after his hunting accident. Few could argue, except, of course, Fignon.

The Frenchman, slightly superior in the mountains, retook the jersey after finishing third on the Alpe d'Huez. And he increased his lead to fifty seconds the following day. The final showdown was reserved for the ultimate time trial, a dramatic twenty-four-and-a-half-kilometer sprint against the clock from Versailles to Paris on the last day.

Logic held that LeMond would regain some time, but the stage would simply be too short to dominate completely. Second place in the Tour would nevertheless constitute a moral victory. But LeMond knew he had nothing to lose. And he raced like it, too. "Don't tell me the splits during the race," he announced to his team director. "I'm planning to go full-out from the gun and maintain for as long as I can. It works or it doesn't. If it doesn't, I'll have nothing to regret. And if it does . . ."

Fignon, in contrast, appeared worried. He had everything to lose, and a pestering saddle sore was becoming a real handicap. Once Fignon was on the road, he never managed to find his rhythm.

LeMond, however, was flying at full tilt. Pushing an enormous fifty-four-by-twelve gearing and benefiting from the newfangled "Scott" triathlete handlebars, which increased his aerodynamic potential, he stormed down the steadily descending road toward Paris. At every time check he was ahead of his French rival. In the end he clocked the fastest time trial in Tour history. Even a decade later, his 54.545 km-an-hour average still stood.

Fignon actually finished the stage a respectable third. But these details are now lost. He also finished fifty-eight seconds behind. And thus, after 3,285 kilometers, he had managed to lose the Tour by a mere eight seconds.

LeMond's reaction was fittingly jubilant. Fignon's was agonizing. For one, the ride represented a renaissance, for the other, demise. LeMond would go on to win another Tour and other major races. Fignon, however, never recuperated from this defeat and was never again a major Tour contender.

But both can be thanked for providing the greatest Tour drama in recent history.

1990: NEAR MISS Perhaps Greg LeMond's worst weakness was his appetite for a good time in the off-season. Needing to distance himself from the confines of the sport, and pained by his separation from his native country, LeMond relished his winter vacations back in Minnesota. And after his stellar 1989 season in which he bounded back to win the Tour and the World Championship, LeMond almost indulged too much.

Returning to Europe visibly overweight and off form, he struggled to find some semblance of fitness. A string of sicknesses didn't help. And as he continued to struggle, he was harpooned by the press. The directors of his Z team were in a panic. The rest of his team was flying, present in all the springtime races. But LeMond floundered. And

after winning the Dauphiné-Libéré, Scottish teammate Robert Millar even joked, "Now all we need is Greg."

But despite the panic, Greg did show up ready to race when the Tour took off on June 30. Well placed near the front after the prologue, LeMond even spent a short spell in the green points jersey, nothing of lasting interest for the American.

But the chance to capture the one jersey he was interested in—the yellow one—was quickly jeopardized when a four-man break grabbed nearly a ten-minute advantage on the opening stage. Few were concerned that Canada's Steve Bauer, Holland's Frans Maassen, or Frenchman Ronan Pensec would threaten the overall title. But Italy's Claudio Chiappucci was an unknown. And as fate would have it, he proved to be LeMond's most lasting threat. The Italian finally slipped into the yellow jersey on the stage-twelve time trial to Villard de Lans. And he was in no hurry to get rid of it.

Forced onto the offensive in the final week, LeMond had to rely on his tactical savvy to slowly chip away at Chiappucci's massive lead. Finally, in the Pyrenees, LeMond narrowed in. On the Luz-Ardiden climb, so crucial in his career, LeMond regained all but five seconds of Chiappucci's lead. Tour victory would be decided in the final time trial. LeMond now had the upper hand. After all, he had already won two Tours in the last time trial. And indeed, in the pursuit race around Vassivière Lake, the Italian proved to be no match for a time-trial specialist like LeMond. At the end of the race, LeMond had spent no more than one day in the *maillot jaune*. But it was the right day—the last day.

DESPITE HIS INHERENT CALM, THERE WAS ALWAYS
PLENTY OF COMMOTION AROUND INDURAIN.

MIGUEL INDURAIN: EL TRANQUILO

MIGUEL INDURAIN, RELAXED AFTER EASILY WINNING THE 1992 RACE.

Like magnets to metal, the cycling world has tried to stick countless nicknames on Miguel Indurain. Big Mig, Mighty Mig, and the Spanish Giant are just some of the monikers used to refer to this cycling legend. And there were a few more. After winning the Alençon time trial in the 1991 Tour he became the Robocop. After his Luxembourg time trial in 1992 he was the Extraterrestrial. And after again flooring the competition in the Bergerac time trial in 1994, his coach, José-Miguel Echavarri, coined the name Tyrano de Bergerac.

For some reason, though, none of these names stuck. Because of Indurain's strange brand of Teflon modesty, such names appeared unfittingly boastful and simply slipped away. But then throughout his reign at the top, Indurain miffed the two-wheeled world. Journalists, frustrated by his timidity, had nothing to report. Many cycling scribes prefer brash champions. At least then they are guaranteed a good quote at the end of the day.

And Indurain's armor proved equally unnerving to his competitors. They were never—through words or action—able to unravel the colossal calm of the Spaniard. Gianni Bugno, also hailed as a

potential Tour champion early in his career, finished with an "Indurain complex." He prematurely left the pool of challengers for the world's biggest bike race. Others, like Claudio Chiappucci, knowing that on the bike they were no match for the Spaniard, contented themselves with cocky quotes to stay in the spotlight.

But really, the only fitting nickname for Indurain would have simply been *el tranquilo*. Throughout his long career and many victories, Indurain always kept his feet planted on planet earth. Never once did he appear to be the victim of his own glory. Actually, Indurain was never much more than a farm boy from northern Spain. And at the end of his career—despite his superstar reputation—he remained very much a country gentleman, albeit a much richer one.

And as it turned out, his farming instincts came in handy in bike racing.

"I come from farming country, and the people who work the earth have taught me a lot," he said in an interview near the end of his career. "You plant, you harvest, you wait for good weather. It's

a philosophy that has served me well in cycling. First you must work the soil, then plant the seeds, then wait, but always working while you wait." Instead of olives and grapes, however, Indurain harvested five Tour de France victories, two Tour of Italy wins, a World Championship title, and an Olympic gold medal.

Ironically, though, in those early years few saw in Miguel Indurain a future Tour de France winner. Power, he had plenty of, but logic held that his immense 196-pound frame would surely handicap him in the mountains. Through a long apprenticeship, however, Big Mig slimmed down and suddenly became a contender.

Already in the 1990 Tour, many considered him a serious threat to Greg LeMond. But Indurain was still a support rider for Spanish hero Pedro Delgado, and he lost crucial time sacrificing himself for his leader.

In 1991, he demonstrated that he was ready to reap what he had sown. Indurain was given the green light, and he quickly made his presence known. Dismantling defending champion Greg

LAURENT JALABERT ON HIS WAY TO HIS MEMORABLE BASTILLE DAY VICTORY DURING THE 1995 TOUR.

THE VOLATILE FRENCH RIDER LUC LEBLANC HAD AN UP YEAR IN 1994. WEEKS AFTER FINISHING FOURTH IN THE TOUR, HE WAS CROWNED WORLD CHAMPION.

DENMARK'S BJARNE RIIS FIRST SHOWED HIS TRUE COLORS BY FINISHING THIRD IN 1995.

LeMond in the Pyrenees, the Spaniard showed that his gigantic build—now a trim 176 pounds—no longer posed problems in the mountains. And by winning the final time trial, he demonstrated that he had lost none of his immense power either.

Once at the summit of the sport, he remained there with rocklike stability for the next five years. With his immense power, one title after another seemed almost to fall in his lap. When he raced to win, he left little suspense.

And yet, he never appeared a slave to success. Returning to his hotel in his team car during the 1995 Tour, Miguel was surprised to find a 100 franc note offered to him in one of his fan mail envelopes. According to Indurain's personal manager Francis LaFarge, who was driving the car, the fan was likely requesting a piece of autographed memorabilia from the Tour winner.

Farther down the road, the gentle giant was solicited at a stoplight by a panhandler with little apparent recognition of his potential client. Miguel, in a saintly manner, handed his stunned onlooker the same bill he had only moments before received.

Clearly Indurain is one of those rare individuals who is just plain satisfied. "I'm basically content with life," insists Indurain. "I just try to keep things in perspective and not get bent out of shape about things." Perhaps this contentment prohibited him from winning even more races.

Who can forget the historic stage to Sestrières, Italy, in the 1992 Tour de France? Although Italy's

Claudio Chiappucci had been on a breakaway for nearly the entire stage, he never possessed a decisive advantage over the chase group. Interestingly, it was not his Spanish rival but Chiappucci's compatriots who led the charge after the feisty Italian. When Indurain's team director José-Miguel Echavarri drove up to ask Indurain if he didn't want to contribute to sealing the fate of the breakaway, the modest Spaniard simply shrugged and declined. "Claudio's been out front all day. He deserves to win. Let him win." And win he did, taking the Tour's most spectacular stage and with it much of the celebration away from Miguel. From Miguel's perspective the hype of heroics mattered little, and it was only the honor of the Tour's yellow jersey that registered.

With similar generosity he gave up his best chance to win the World Championship in 1995, content

MARCO PANTANI'S ALPE D'HUEZ STAGE IN 1995 WOULD NOT BE HIS LAST.

BJARNE RIIS POWERS TOWARD TOUR VICTORY IN 1996 ON THE SWELTERING STAGE TO INDURAIN'S HOMETOWN, PAMPLONA, SPAIN.

to work for his countryman Abraham Olano. So what if he was the strongman in the race?

Unlike cycling's winningest champion, Eddy Merckx, Miguel would never be nicknamed the Cannibal. He simply had too much of the *tranquilo* in him. Perhaps, though, such generosity and unpretentiousness were essential to bike racing in the 1990s. Cycling had changed greatly since the days of Merckx and Hinault. The difference between the water bottle carriers and winners often became minimal. Cycling's fin de siècle spirit favored consensus. Brashness can now be beaten down easily by the mass of increasingly talented riders. Arrogance no longer has its place in the modern world of cycling. Great champions like

Indurain needed a hearty dose of discretion. One could still hammer the competition to a pulp, but only in a gentlemanly manner.

Almost unnervingly, Indurain's victims—be it the cocky Chiappucci or the calculated Tony Rominger—were always "dignified," always "worthy" opponents, according to Indurain. And after a while, some of them almost seemed to take pleasure in losing to him. "I came in second to Indurain. That's as good as winning," more than one loser could be heard saying.

Indurain's unprecedented five consecutive Tour victories are in no small part due to that same sense of calm, a calm that saved him from selling out and that saved him from wasting any unneces-

sary energy on the relentless attacks of his opponents. Indeed, if Indurain shares one quality with Tour predecessor Greg LeMond, it is his tactical sense. Both had that uncanny sense never to buckle under pressure. This quality helped make both of them the dominant riders of their generation.

Going into the 1996 Tour, Indurain appeared as strong as ever. But as the three-week race revealed, he was not. And when Bjarne Riis finally did break him that year, Indurain quietly accepted his defeat, well aware that the end of his tenure at the top was inevitable.

And fittingly, with similar discretion, he retired at the end of that same year.

DESPITE THE WEATHER, THERE WAS NOTHING FOGGY ABOUT INDURAIN'S FIFTH STRAIGHT TOUR VICTORY.

1991–1996: THE INDURAIN YEARS

DESPITE TWO WORLD CHAMPIONSHIP TITLES, GIANNI BUGNO DEVELOPED A MENTAL BLOCK IN THE TOUR. SOME CALLED IT HIS "INDURAIN COMPLEX."

ALTHOUGH EXHAUSTED, SWITZERLAND'S ALEX ZÜLLE WAS HAVING HIS BEST TOUR RIDE IN 1995.

Spain has never been in need of climbers. There are plenty of Spanish eagles of the mountains. But time trialers are a definite rarity. Not until Miguel Indurain matured could his country boast an all-around champion of such stature. He could climb, sure. He wouldn't be Spanish if he couldn't. But time trialing was his specialty. And like the first five-time Tour winner, Jacques Anquetil, the race against the clock was the key to all five of the Spaniard's Tour victories.

1991: INDURAIN YEAR ONE
At first glance Greg LeMond looked to be in a perfect position to defend his Tour title in 1991. After the first stage he had temporarily slipped into the yellow jersey, and throughout the opening week was never far from the lead. But once again, the American's shaky pre-Tour preparations caused him to unravel. In the Tour of Italy, he had failed to match any of the top climbers, and the Tour de France proved to be more of the same.

On the first mountain stage into Jaca, Spain, LeMond already showed signs of cracking, and then on the pivotal stage from Jaca to Val Louron,

he folded, losing over seven minutes to mountain goats like Miguel Indurain and Claudio Chiappucci.

Back in 1986, LeMond lost over five minutes to Bernard Hinault in a single stage and still recovered to win the race. But circumstances had changed. He was no longer a bright young champion budding with strength, but an ill-trained, aging champion who still carried several shotgun pellets in the lining of his heart from his hunting accident. But like all natural-born champions, LeMond had so much class on his bike that any vulnerabilities were well hidden.

Miguel Indurain was also well hidden going into the 1991 race. He had finished tenth the year before, but in 1990 his only ambition had been to ride support for team leader and 1988 Tour champion Pedro Delgado. If all the time Indurain sacrificed in deference to his leader in 1990 were calculated, it would show that the young Spaniard could have been at or very near the top of the rankings. But before 1991, Indurain's potential could only be estimated by calculations and hypotheses. He had yet to win a major Tour.

When Indurain won 1991's stage-eight time trial from Argentan to Alençon, eyes began to open. Indurain was suddenly a true contender, and when he disposed of LeMond in the Pyrenees, the Spanish Giant became a force to reckon with. Italians Gianni Bugno and Claudio Chiappucci tried: Bugno was consistently strong but consistently second to Indurain, and all Chiappucci could do was to prove that his 1990 Tour ride had not been a fluke. He eventually finished third, over five minutes behind. By the time the race returned to Paris, the Indurain era had been born.

1992: INDURAIN YEAR TWO
Before the start of the 1992 Tour, Greg LeMond warned Miguel Indurain that it is much easier to win a first Tour than to defend it. The American knew what he was talking about—he had already won three. How would the introverted Spaniard handle the pressure of being the defending Tour de France champ? Perfectly well, thank you. Although unheralded youngsters like Richard Virenque and Pascal Lino shared the yellow jersey during the opening week, Indurain wasted little time in showing that he was once again up to snuff. First he won the opening Prologue,

COLOMBIA'S ALVARO MEJIA NEARLY FINISHED ON THE PARIS PODIUM IN 1993, FINALLY SLIPPING TO FOURTH IN THE LAST TIME TRIAL.

and then in the first true test—a sixty-five-kilometer time trial in Luxembourg—Indurain sucked nearly all the suspense from the race. He steamrolled the hilly terrain at nearly forty-nine kilometers an hour, leaving top challengers like Gianni Bugno, Claudio Chiappucci, Erik Breukink, and LeMond between four and six minutes behind.

Officially, Lino still held the yellow jersey, but his lead, which once stood at six minutes, could now be counted in seconds. His days were clearly numbered. And when Indurain slipped into the lead in the Alps, all yellow-jersey conversation came to a close. Now only scrapping for stage wins could offer consolation to the rest of the pack.

Although the overall race was padlocked for Indurain, the rest of the Tour's top men continued to perform admirably: Chiappucci had his greatest day yet by winning the stage into Sestrières in his native Italy; American climber Andy Hampsten finally won a much-deserved mountain stage up Alpe d'Huez; and 1987 Tour winner Stephen Roche served up his swan song by taking the stage into La Bourboule. Only LeMond came up empty-handed. Despite his hopes to return to the top of the Tour charts, he dropped out early on stage fourteen, well before Indurain rolled into Paris for his second consecutive win.

1993: INDURAIN YEAR THREE Miguel Indurain's toughest Tour challenge came in the form of Switzerland's Tony Rominger in 1993. Unfortunately, Tony Rominger realized too late that he could have captured the overall win. "I only came here to win the polka-dot jersey and a couple of stages," he said after the race was over. And that he did quite nicely.

As soon as the race entered the Alps, Rominger drove the pace, winning back-to-back stages at Serre-Chevalier and at Isola 2000. But before the mountains had even started, Rominger had lost over four minutes, not to mention two teammates. In the Pyrenees Rominger again went to the front, constantly testing Indurain—although it has to be said that the Spaniard always responded.

And then on the final time trial Rominger managed the impossible. He handed Indurain his first Tour time-trial defeat in three years. Because of Rominger's constant threats, Indurain faded in the last week, and he finished the Tour so exhausted that he bypassed many of the post-Tour criteriums. In 1993, though, Rominger and the rest had come to the race believing that Indurain was invincible, and they realized too late that he might have been broken.

1994: INDURAIN YEAR FOUR The phrase "a state of grace" pretty much encapsulates Indurain's 1994 Tour performance. Although Tony Rominger was pitted as the chief rival before the race, after the first time trial in the French Perigord region, Indurain no longer had rivals. As in Luxembourg in 1992, the Spaniard humiliated the field. For the next eleven days Indurain just sat back and controlled the race. But as soon as the race hit the mountains, he served notice that he would be no chump once the roads went up. On the supersteep finish to Hautacam outside of Lourdes, Indurain's Banesto team went to the front and dropped most

of their opponents. And when the three-time defending Tour winner finally took control at the front, only France's Luc Leblanc could follow. Although Leblanc came away with the stage win, the damage had already been done; no one could question Indurain's authority.

The rest of the race was given over to some fresh faces. The young climber Richard Virenque finally won a major mountain stage, as well as the first of four best-climber jerseys he has claimed in his career. Obscure Russian veteran Piotr Ugrumov became the first Eastern European rider to finish on the podium (in second place), and Italian up-and-comer Marco Pantani provided hints that he would soon be a dominant force in the mountains.

1995: INDURAIN YEAR FIVE Indurain came to the race in 1995 ready to win an unprecedented fifth straight Tour de France. Sure, Jacques Anquetil, Eddy Merckx, and Bernard Hinault were all members of the five-up club, but none of them was able to do it in consecutive years.

Although spectacular crashes by Chris Boardman and Laurent Jalabert captured the headlines during the opening week, Indurain stayed out of trouble. He kept a low profile but never strayed from the front rows of the pack.

Then on the stage to Liège, Indurain offered one of the great surprises of his career. Nearing the finish, he bolted off the front and simply dropped his chief rivals. American rider Lance Armstrong had a front-row seat for Indurain's attack, and nobody was more impressed: "Man, I was right there. I was right on his wheel. But when he accelerated there

AT THE MIDI-LIBRE RACE ONLY WEEKS BEFORE THE 1996 TOUR, RIIS SHOWED HE WAS READY TO RACE.

was nothing I could do! I just watched him ride away." Only Belgium's Johan Bruyneel—who was already up the road when Indurain attacked—could follow as the Spaniard charged through the last twenty-five kilometers to Liège. Bruyneel even managed to sprint around the Spanish great for the stage win and a temporary taste of the yellow jersey—but everyone knew that the real winner that day was Indurain.

Justice was served the next day, when Big Mig took the race's first time trial and recuperated his familiar yellow jersey. Some were surprised that he only managed to win by twelve seconds over Denmark's Bjarne Riis, but Indurain defended himself thus: "I just rode two time trials in two days [the time trial and his 25-kilometer solo flight to Liège the previous day] so it is normal that I'd be a little tired on the second day." Few could argue.

On the stage to La Plagne—the first mountain stage in the Tour—the Spaniard dominated his competition. Switzerland's Alex Zülle may have grabbed the stage win, but he was too far down in the overall rankings to be considered a real threat. And as Indurain led the race's top contenders to the line, rivals like Tony Rominger and Richard Virenque took a backseat ride on the Indurain engine.

After his performance in the Alps, Indurain was sitting pretty. No one thought that anyone would be stealing the yellow jersey anytime soon, but French star Laurent Jalabert had a surprise in store for his Spanish rival. It came on Bastille Day, the French national holiday. Jalabert and a handful of his ONCE teammates attacked early on the stage from Saint-Étienne to Mende, immediately splitting the field. Suddenly Indurain was isolated, as most of his Banesto teammates had been caught sleeping. While Indurain tried to

regroup his troops, Jalabert and company were off and running. "Indurain was definitely very scared," remembered American rider Frankie Andreu, who managed to make the front group. "He was looking all around for help."

By the time help came, Jalabert was already wearing the yellow jersey on the road. With nearly a ten-minute advantage, the stage was clearly lost. But after a long, wretched pursuit, Indurain managed to cut his losses and save his shirt. For the French, though, Jalabert gave his compatriots one of the most memorable Tour performances in recent history.

DEATH IN THE PYRENEES For all practical purposes the 1995 Tour came to a halt after the tragic death of Italy's Fabio Casartelli in a freak downhill pileup on the stage from St. Gaudens to Cauterets, nobody

AMERICAN LANCE ARMSTRONG FINISHES HIS FIRST TOUR, ONE THAT INCLUDED THE DEATH OF A TEAMMATE AS WELL AS A STAGE WIN.

ALTHOUGH HE FINISHED TENTH, SWITZERLAND'S TONY ROMINGER WAS CLEARLY AT THE END OF HIS CAREER IN 1996.

felt much like racing. All professional bikers know they are not exactly in a low-risk profession. They spend most of their careers in a high-speed blur, not fully conscious of the inherent dangers. But when one of their own dies, the void they feel is unimaginable, and each of them is given a poignant slap in the face to remind them of their vulnerability. The racing stagnated after Casartelli's death. And why not? The general classification had already been locked up. So with uncharacteristic lethargy, the pack ambled back to Paris, and Indurain's victory, perhaps his greatest, was over-shadowed by tragedy.

1996: NOT INDURAIN YEAR SIX

Who, before the start of the 1996 Tour, would have bet against five-time Tour winner Miguel Indurain? The Spanish Giant had followed the same preparation as the one that led him to his fifth victory, and he appeared just as unstoppable as in the five previous editions. In his last major test, the Dauphiné-Libéré, Indurain virtually single-handedly (or -leggedly) dropped all his rivals on the legendary Izoard climb. A history-making sixth Tour victory seemed likely.

But a three-week race doesn't always lend itself to logic. And the 1996 Tour held plenty of surprises. The biggest, however, came from Indurain himself, who faltered early in the mountains and never regained his composure.

Perhaps the only noticeable difference going into the 1996 race was that Indurain was carrying a few superfluous kilograms when the race started in Holland. Under normal circumstances, he would have had ample time to shed the extra weight in the opening week. But incessant rains—and then snow—got in the way. Instead of a high-liquid diet favored in the heat, cold rains require high caloric intake. And although the extra calories ensure insulation, they also build mass—the one thing Indurain did not need.

Indurain paid a heavy price as soon as the race hit the mountains on the stage from Chambery to Les Arcs. Top riders like Laurent Jalabert and Alex Zülle dropped and crashed out respectively, and in the final kilometers of the final climb to Les Arcs, Indurain's number was finally up.

He hoped to rebound, but the Spaniard was clearly not the climber he once was. To the newly crowned king, Denmark's Bjarne Riis, Indurain lost three minutes and twenty-three seconds at Les Arcs; twenty-eight seconds on the climb to Sestrières; two minutes and twenty-eight seconds to the finish on the Hautacam; and eight minutes and thirty seconds on the most grueling mountain stage of all, which happened to terminate at his hometown of Pamplona.

"We prepared everything to the most exacting detail," explained his long-time director José-Miguel Echavarri. "We rode virtually the same races, but never in a hundred years did we consider the idea of snow in July." But as Echavarri surely knew, nothing is ever sure in cycling.

A PRODUCT OF THE EAST GERMAN SPORTS INSTITUTE, JAN ULLRICH WAS TRAINED TO SUFFER. DESPITE PLENTY OF CRASHES, THE TWENTY-TWO-YEAR-OLD MANAGED TO WIN A STAGE AND FINISH SECOND OVERALL IN 1996. NOT BAD FOR A FIRST TIMER.

TOWARD THE CENTENNIAL: PANTANI, ULLRICH, ARMSTRONG, AND BEYOND

PANTANI IS UP THE ROAD, BUT ULLRICH POWERS HIS WAY TOWARD ALPE D'HUEZ AND SAVES HIS YELLOW SHIRT IN 1997.

At the end of every great reign, cycling contains a power struggle, as different riders attempt to become the new patron of the peloton. One of cycling's most redeeming aspects is its ability to constantly reinvent itself. Fresh faces and new stars seem to assure such things.

After Miguel Indurain suddenly retired from the sport on the heels of his unexpected Tour de France defeat in 1996, the void left by him was vast. Certainly Denmark's Bjarne Riis was in no position to become the new chief. At thirty-two, he was already more than three months older than Indurain when he won the Tour in 1996. And when he lost his title defense the following year, few were surprised.

Riis, however, owned some insurance. And it came in the form of his young German teammate Jan Ullrich. Ullrich was only twenty-two when he was

called up to help out Riis in 1996. And help out he did. After doing a lion's share of the teamwork he managed to win the final time trial and to finish second overall. Instantly he was heralded as the king of the new generation. He quickly confirmed in 1997, winning the Tour by nearly ten minutes over climber Richard Virenque—one of the greatest winning margins in recent history.

But almost as quickly, Ullrich showed that, unlike his Spanish successor, he was not infallible. After his 1997 victory, he let himself get bogged down in off-season protocol festivities. Overweight and off form, he never established the needed base for a three-week affair like the Tour. And he paid for it in the Alps.

As with Indurain in 1996, poor weather proved to be his unraveling. And on the rain-soaked stage from

Grenoble to Deux Alpes, Ullrich simply could not respond to recent Tour of Italy winner Marco Pantani. Pantani, of course, went on to win the stage as well as the 1998 race.

But while Pantani and Ullrich appeared to be two of the top riders of their generation, they also proved to be two of the most troubled. Less than a year after his memorable Tour victory, the man once considered the savior of the 1998 race soon found trouble of his own. Well on his way to a second Tour of Italy race, Pantani was suddenly ousted only days from the finish when he failed to pass a blood test. The downfall of the cyclist formerly know as the "Pirate" was swift yet complete. In fact, since his 1999 Tour of Italy demise, Pantani has spent more time in and out of courtrooms than he has racing his bike. He has

AFTER NEARLY A WEEK IN THE YELLOW JERSEY, FRENCH TEAM RIDER CÈDRIC VASSEUR WON THE HEARTS OF HIS COMPATRIOTS IN THE 1997 TOUR.

A MAJESTIC MARCO PANTANI GRIMACES TOWARD HIS SECOND ALPE D'HUEZ TRIUMPH IN 1997.

JAN ULLRICH HAS LEARNED A THING OR TWO ABOUT THE PRESSURE OF THE YELLOW JERSEY. IN 1998 HE CRACKED UNDER ITS WEIGHT.

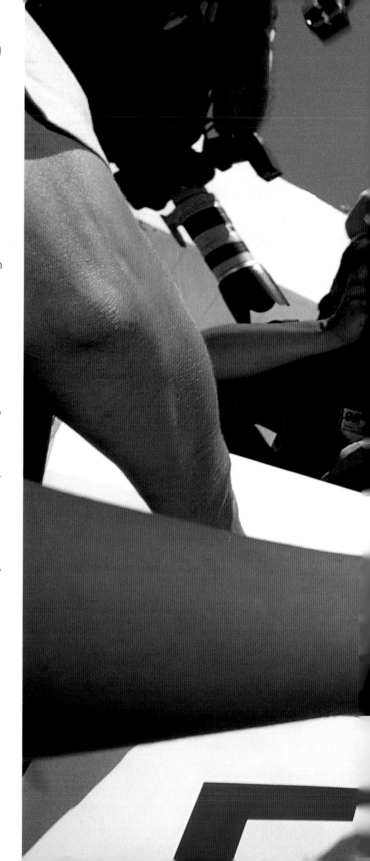

been charged with sporting fraud for a number of incidents throughout his career.

In a strangely similar setback, Ullrich has fought weight and injury problems since his magnificent 1997 Tour. And when he tested positive for recreational drugs in an out-of-competition control in 2002, it became clear that the German had his own set of personal issues to resolve. Still, despite his many detours, he has managed to finish second four times in the past seven years.

America's Bobby Julich proved to be one of the best American stage racers since Greg LeMond. After finishing third in the 1998 Tour, he looked to be on his way to Tour glory.

But before Julich could confirm, another American has taken center stage. Until the 1999 Tour de France, few considered Lance Armstrong a serious Tour contender. Sure, he became one of the youngest world champions in the history of the sport back in 1993, but he simply appeared too limited in the high mountains for the Tour. And after being diagnosed with testicular cancer, few thought he would ever ride a bike again, let alone race in the Tour de France.

Armstrong, however, always rides at his best when he is riding against the odds. And with the odds stacked against him, the Texan once again rose to the occasion. Equaling greats like Jacques Anquetil, Eddy Merckx, Bernard Hinault and Miguel Indurain, Armstrong won every time trial in the 1999 race. And when he added the mountain stage to Sestrières, the rest of the field pretty much resigned themselves to racing for second place. Of course,

previous Tour winners like Ullrich and Pantani both opted out of the 1999 event. But if Armstrong couldn't be beat by cancer, one wonders if any cyclist could have surpassed him in his quest for Tour glory.

With Armstrong now on the verge of joining Anquetil, Merckx, Hinault, and Indurain as five-time winners, what riders in his shadow seem primed to take over as Tour winner one day soon?

It's a simple question with a clouded answer, as no one currently stands out. Spain's Joseba Beloki, third in 2000 and 2001 and second in 2002, is best positioned. But will his time trialing ever be good enough to actually win the race? His countryman Igor Gonzalez de Galdeano has the opposite problem—he's a good time trialer, but he's not so good at climbing. Colombian Santiago Botero, who beat Armstrong in both a time trial and mountain stage in the 2002 Tour, climbs and time trials well—but not consistently. A host of younger riders, including Scotland's David Millar, Australia's Cadel Evans, Italy's Ivan Basso, and Spain's Oscar Sevilla, still lack the experience to climb the top step of the Tour podium.

On paper, Germany's Jan Ullrich still possesses the most complete package and, two years younger than Armstrong, is still young enough to win again. But will he ever regain the concentration needed to win the world's greatest bike race?

One thing is certain. When it comes to the Tour de France, the candidates are many. But the winners are few.

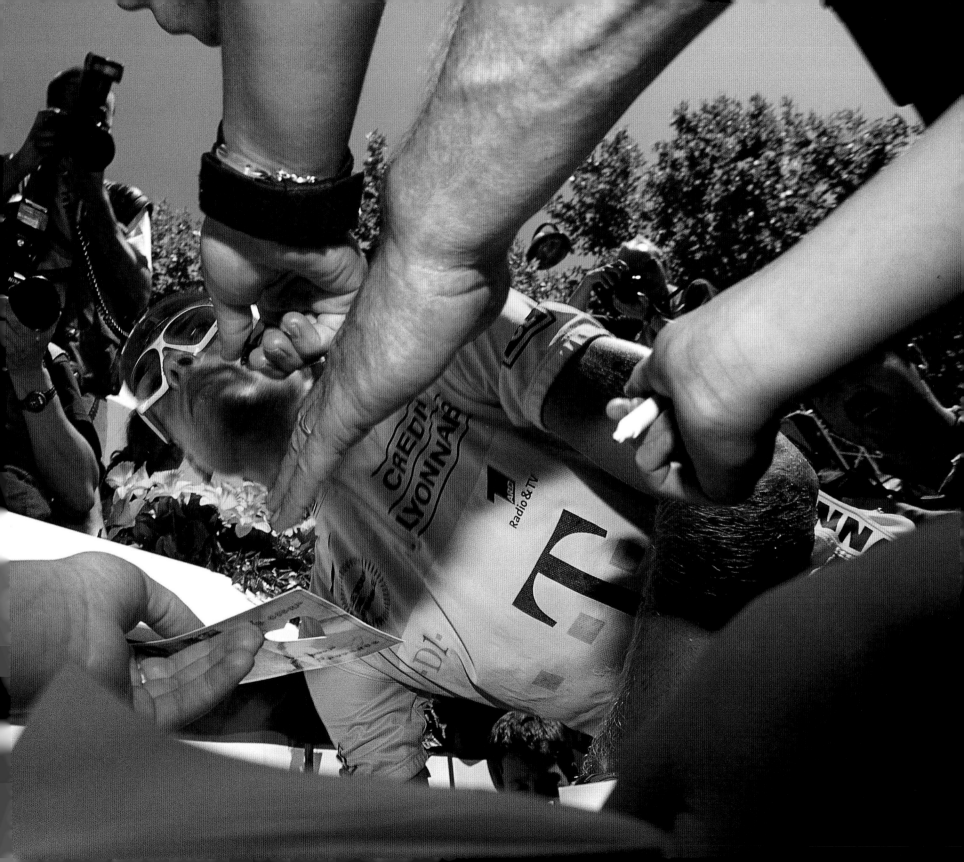

STUART O'GRADY KEPT THE AUSTRALIAN TOUR TRADITION ALIVE WITH A SPELL IN YELLOW IN 1998. HE PROMISES IT WON'T BE THE LAST TIME HE ATTRACTS ATTENTION ON THE BIKE.

ALTHOUGH ULLRICH RODE STRONGLY IN THE PYRENEES, INSIDERS ALREADY UNDERSTOOD THAT HE WAS BEATABLE IN 1998.

PANTANI FIRST SHOWED THAT A CLIMBER COULD AGAIN WIN THE TOUR WHEN HE CHARGED AWAY FROM JAN ULLRICH ON THE PLÂTEAU DE BEILLE CLIMB IN THE PYRENEES DURING THE 1998 RACE.

AFTER HELPING ARMSTRONG WIN THE 1999 TOUR, THE U.S. POSTAL SERVICE TEAM HAD A RIGHT TO BE PATRIOTIC ONCE THEY FINISHED IN PARIS.

TEXAS FLOOD HITS
THE TOUR

TYLER HAMILTON PROVED TO BE A TIRELESS SUPPORT RIDER FOR ARMSTRONG IN THE 1999 TOUR.

After the drug-dominated debacle that was the 1998 Tour, race organizers pitched the 1999 event as the "Tour of Renewal." And they got one with the stunning victory by Lance Armstrong—that ragin' Texan who was going through his own renewal after recovering from testicular cancer in 1996.

The pre-cancer Armstrong was a great single-day racer. After winning the World Championship in only his second season as a professional, he went on to win such prestigious classics as Belgium's Fléche-Wallonne and Spain's Classica San Sebastian. But in his own words, "The Tour de France was another beast altogether."

Post-cancer Armstrong was a leaner, meaner champion, and one who was now unintimidated by the world's greatest bike race. Climbing and time trialing were no longer weak points, and after finishing fourth in the 1998 Tour of Spain—like the Tour de France, a three-week race—Armstrong finally understood he could be a Tour contender.

When the 1999 Tour started, Armstrong immediately showed his opponents that he would be a serious competitor. After winning the opening Prologue, he went on to win the Metz time trial, a 56.5-kilometer VO2 Max-blast. Finishing well behind were such chrono specialists as Switzerland's Alex Zülle and world time-trial champion Abraham Olano of Spain.

Then, on the first mountain day to Sestrières, Armstrong powered away from challengers like Zülle and Fernando Escartin of Spain. After controlling his opponents for the next two weeks, he won the final time trial in Futuroscope, thus equaling greats like Jacques Anquetil, Eddy Merckx, and Miguel Indurain by taking every race against the clock in the same year.

Armstrong's dominance, however, has not come without a price. On the heels of the drug scandals that tainted the 1998 Tour, some fans, especially in France, the cradle of the tour, appeared skeptical of his miraculous comeback and sudden emergence as a Tour dominator. Armstrong's second victory in 2000 was then tainted when French authorities opened a formal investigation on his U.S. Postal Service team for suspicion of doping—although nothing was proven.

His third Tour, too, suffered when Armstrong announced to the general public that he was working with Italy's Dr. Ferrari, one of the sport's most-suspected doctors on the doping front, who has been implicated in several high-profile investigations for incitation of illegal drugs in sport as well as sporting fraud. Armstrong nevertheless defended his right to choose whom he worked with. Confident Ferrari would eventually be cleared, Armstrong insisted that he never witnessed any wrongdoing and underlined that, despite the accusations, Ferrari remained one of the sport's top technicians.

Armstrong seems to accept, although uncomfortably, the suspicion as part of the terrain of a champion in sport today. "The champions, the record breakers, the best will never be vindicated," he has said. "There's always going to be somebody that says, 'no, I don't believe it.' You see it every day."

Only in Armstrong's fourth Tour win in 2002, his most dominant, did the constant criticism subside. Perhaps critics realized that, suspicion or not, Armstrong had become one of the most consistently dominant champions in the history of the sport.

No Tour champion has won four Tours without a fifth, and of the other five-time winners only Eddy Merckx and Bernard Hinault compare to Armstrong in their ability to destroy the field in either mountains or time trials.

How long will the reign of the American last? Perhaps only he knows. For the moment, however, no rival complete with all the needed skills of a Tour winner is visible, and Armstrong may well be the first rider to break the five-time Tour barrier.

ITALY'S MARIO CIPOLLINI GOT OFF TO A SLOW START IN THE 1999 TOUR,
BUT FINISHED BY MAKING HISTORY WITH FOUR CONSECUTIVE STAGE WINS.

LANCE ARMSTRONG MAKES CLIMBING LOOK EASY UP THE VAL LOURON-AZET IN THE PYRENEES.

SPANISH NATIONAL CHAMPION ANGEL CASERO PROVIDED ONE OF THE SURPRISES IN THE 1999 TOUR WITH HIS FIFTH-PLACE FINISH.

AFTER THE FUTUROSCOPE TIME TRIAL, ARMSTRONG TRIES TO FATHOM HIS LATEST EXPLOIT. HE HAS JUST BEEN THE FIRST RIDER SINCE MIGUEL INDURAIN TO WIN EVERY TIME TRIAL IN THE TOUR.

RUSSIAN VETERAN DIMITRI KONYSHEV SHOWED HE STILL KNEW HOW TO WIN BIKE RACES AFTER TAKING STAGE 14 INTO SAINT GAUDENS.

KEVIN LIVINGSTON SACRIFICED HIS OWN CHANCES TO HELP HIS FRIEND AND TEAMMATE LANCE ARMSTRONG WIN THE 1999 TOUR.

EVOLUTION OF THE TOUR DE FRANCE BIKE

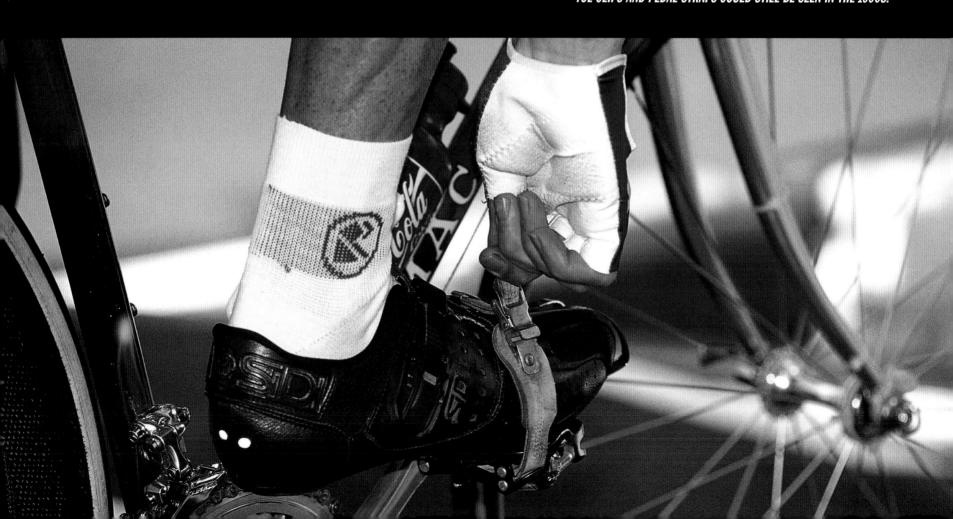

TOE CLIPS AND PEDAL STRAPS COULD STILL BE SEEN IN THE 1990S.

HANDLEBARS AND STEMS—1903 TO 1939

As the bicycle evolved at the beginning of the century, the shape of the handlebars went through its share of changes. Early racing bikes used steel handlebars that varied in bend from the swept-back mustache design to the deep-drop bar used for track sprinting. Most early Tour de France bicycles were equipped with a heavy steel bar that provided a compromise between the different styles. This bar facilitated optimum aerodynamic position yet was comfortable over the long haul. Racing stems were made exclusively from steel until the 1940s, when lighter aluminum models were introduced.

HANDLEBARS AND STEMS—1947 TO THE PRESENT

For the traditional road bike, handlebars and stems have developed little over the past decades. Italian companies like Cinelli, TTT, and Italmanubri dominated the market with aluminum forged stems. Weight has decreased by up to 30 percent and nearly all handlebar manufacturers today experiment with anatomical variations on the drop. The traditional rounded drop, however, remains popular.

Stems have gone through more visible changes, as some are now forged from steel while others are directly mounted onto the fork.

The big breakthrough in handlebar technology came in the 1989 Tour de France when American Greg LeMond mounted a pair of special aerodynamic handlebars onto his time-trial bike. Initially used in triathlons, the "aero bars" helped LeMond forge his legendary eight-second victory. As a result, various "aero bars" have become the norm in all time-trial events.

PEDALS—1903 TO 1939

Already at the start of the first Tour de France the basic pedal system was in use. Early racers used flat pedals that were known as "rat traps" because of their curious shape. A metal toe clip was attached to one side of the platform to keep the ball of the rider's foot in an optimal position and a leather toe strap wrapped around the foot and held it in place.

Early cycling shoes, essentially lightweight oxfords with stiff soles, distributed pressure evenly across the entire foot. Slotted metal cleats hooked into the pedal helped secure the foot.

PEDALS—1947 TO THE PRESENT

Pedal design was revolutionized in the 1980s with the clipless pedal system. The French ski-binding company LOOK developed a one-click pedal system that was both easy and efficient. Although the clipless design was first experimented with in the 1970s, prototypes to the LOOK pedal were clumsy in comparison. Now, with a simple lateral twist of the foot, the shoe is released from the pedal.

Today virtually no road cyclists, and only a small group of track cyclists, still use traditional clip pedals.

SADDLE—1903 TO 1939

Because the saddle is the main contact point between rider and bike, it has gone through countless variations in the search for the optimum compromise between weight and comfort. Early saddles experimented with various forms: two vertical halves with a space down the center, air-cushioned seats, even a toilet-seat saddle, completely open in the center.

By far the most popular early saddle was the "hammock" saddle, which stretched leather tightly over a steel frame. J. B. Brooks invented this legendary saddle, and it is still a popular choice, although rarely among professionals.

SADDLE—1947 TO THE PRESENT

While the leather hammock saddle remains one of the most efficient designs on the market, it does have one major drawback—it requires a long break-in period.

Synthetic alternatives have provided a hoard of advances over the past few decades. Today the frames of saddles are made of aluminum, titanium, or carbon fiber and are then joined with a plastic shell and covered with a thin layer of natural leather. The many currently existing models all vary in some way. Some add synthetic gels to increase cushioning. Others offer pressure-relieving holes. But today, nearly every rider—regardless of their build—can find a comfortable option.

FRAME—1903 TO 1939

At the turn of the twentieth century, the diamond-frame bicycle became the acknowledged standard for comfort and light weight. The frame used seven or eight tubes and looked like two adjoined triangles. Virtually all diamond-frame bikes used steel tubes.

First developed by the Humber Corporation in 1888, it has since proved to be about the biggest breakthrough for bikes since the wheel.

FRAME—1947 TO THE PRESENT

Since World War II the diamond-frame bicycle has remained the standard. The choice of material, however, never ceases to evolve. Steel tubes still offer an intelligent compromise between stiffness, weight, and durability. Aluminum, titanium, and carbon fiber have become increasingly popular.

Superstiff aluminum tubes were first introduced in the late 1970s and have since gained widespread popularity for their solid, stiff ride. Advanced titanium alloys offer a light, supple, corrosion-resistant option, despite its customer-unfriendly cost.

Composite materials, namely carbon fiber, have become increasingly popular since they offer stiffness, lightness, and longevity at pocketbook-friendly prices. In addition, a new generation of metal-matrix (mixtures of metal and nonmetallic materials) offers even more options.

BRAKES—1903 TO 1939

Needless to say, braking is nearly as important as pedaling, and although track cyclists dispense with brakes, for the Tour cyclist, they are rather indispensable. During the early twentieth century, braking options varied from the drum brake to disc brakes to internal hub brakes. But the unanimous choice of Tour riders has been the cable-controlled, side-pull brakes. With the lever attached to the handlebar, cyclists can slow down and stop easily.

Over the years several brake-pad materials have been used. But because of its effeciency and durability, rubber is the logical choice.

BRAKES—1947 TO THE PRESENT

Until the 1990s, traditional side-pull brakes were commonly used by most riders. Although center-pull brake designs were used in the 1970s and later in the 1980s, they have never become the popular choice in the Tour de France. In the 1990s, however, a variation of the side-pull design generally took over. Today the dual-pivot brakes from Shimano and Campagnolo dominate the market.

Undoubtedly, the brake lever has gone through the greatest changes. In 1991 Shimano introduced the STI brake-lever system, which integrated both the brake and shift levers into a single unit. Despite the added weight on the front end of the bicycle, the ability to shift and brake simultaneously has proven to be one of the century's greatest racing revolutions.

DRIVE TRAIN—1903 TO 1939

Before the Tour began, the bicycle industry produced crude rear derailleurs, which moved the chain from cog to cog. But such systems were considered recreational gadgets, and Tour cyclists were forbidden to use them until the 1930s. But since 1937, the year the Tour ban ended, derailleurs have been an integral part of the racing machine.

DRIVE TRAIN—1947 TO THE PRESENT

In the 1950s front and rear derailleurs, mounted on the frame, became standard fare. Derailleurs are connected to shift levers by cables. Some manufacturers have experimented with electronic shift levers, but they have not yet found widespread use.

With two front chain rings and five cogs on the rear freewheel, cyclists had ten gearing options. Eventually six-, seven-, eight-, and nine-speed freewheels were introduced, giving riders up to eighteen possible gear combinations. Riders have occasionally experimented with a third chain ring as well. But real men, it seems, don't need an inner ring.

WHEEL—1903 TO 1939

Throughout the history of the Tour, the spoked bicycle wheel has remained a fundamental part of the machine. In 1924 Tullio Campagnolo facilitated wheel changes with the quick-release hub.

Clincher tires—held to the rim by a wire bead—have been used with inner tubes since the nineteenth century. But bike racers preferred tubular tires, a one-piece inner tube and tire glued to the rim. Although more costly, they proved more responsive.

WHEEL—1947 TO THE PRESENT

Although the spoked bicycle wheel remains popular at all levels, the wheel has changed significantly in the last forty-five years. Rims can weigh as little as 250 grams and are made from lightweight, heat-treated aluminum or carbon fiber. Rims vary in width and depth depending on the desired strength or aerodynamic preferences.

For time trialing, disc wheels are used frequently. Usually made from carbon fiber and kevlar composite, semidisc wheels now tend to be preferred. These wheels, with three or four spokes, maintain the aerodynamic advantage of full discs but are more efficient in crosswinds.

And the clincher tire has gone through its own renaissance. Now, virtually matching tubulars for weight, responsiveness, and durability, many professionals ride clinchers instead of the traditional tubular.

"GINO THE PIOUS" WAS NOW "GINO THE OLD." BUT SOON TOUR RIDERS WOULD NO LONGER HAVE GINO TO KICK AROUND ANYMORE. ITALIAN LEGEND GINO BARTALI WAITS PATIENTLY BEFORE A STAGE START OF THE 1953 TOUR, HIS LAST.

UNFORTUNATELY FOR RICHARD VIRENQUE, THE CHARISMATIC FRENCH STAR ATTRACTED MORE ATTENTION OFF THE BIKE THROUGH HIS INVOLVEMENT IN THE "FESTINA AFFAIR" THAN HE EVER DID ON THE BIKE.

DRUGS IN SPORTS: THE NOT-SO-STRAIGHT DOPE

HONESTY HAS ITS PRICE. ALTHOUGH BERNARD THÉVENET CAME CLEAN ON DRUG USE, HE WAS BLACK LISTED BY HIS COLLEAGUES.

To dope or not to dope: that is the question. And it has been around nearly as long as cycling. In the early days of the sport—what many considered kinder, gentler days—drugs and sport seemed worlds apart. But there weren't any drug controls back then. Society's view of drug use in general was less critical—not to mention more naive. Even Coca-Cola boasted cocaine as a root ingredient.

Cyclists themselves spoke more openly about drugs. Already in the 1924 Tour, the legendary Pélissier brothers blasted at the inherent vices of the sport. After dropping out in protest to a ruling by Tour director Henri Desgrange, they revealed to Albert Londres, then serving as a journalist for *Le Petit Parisien:*

"You want to see how we ride [the Tour de France]? Here . . . This is cocaine for the eyes, and chloroform for the gums . . . This is ointment to warm the knees. And pills? You want to see pills?"

They each pulled out three containers.

"In short," said Francis, "We ride with dynamite." Henri continued, "You haven't seen the showers at the finish? That's worth a trip. The stained mud, white like shrouds. The diarrhea empties us . . . And our toenails, I lost six of the ten. They just fall off progressively each stage. And you haven't seen anything yet. Just wait till we hit the Pyrenees. That's hard labor."

Londres's story appeared as the scoop of the century. But rather than bring about change, it simply defined a tendency—that of the willingness of some to take performance-enhancing drugs.

And with conveyor-belt regularity drug scandals return nearly every decade.

When rising French hope Roger Rivière crashed out of the 1960 Tour, paralyzed for life, amphetamines were found in his jersey pockets. Similar substances were found in the blood of British rider Tom Simpson when he collapsed from his bike on Mont Ventoux and died in 1967.

A decade later, French champion Bernard Thévenet was hospitalized after winning his second Tour de France in 1977. Later that winter, he admitted that cortisone abuse had rotted his liver. He was one of the lucky ones. He raced again, although never at his previous level.

And in 1988, Spaniard Pedro Delgado was nearly suspended from the Tour while wearing the yellow jersey. Masking drugs were found in his body. Only through a technicality was he allowed to continue racing and win the race; the particular drug was banned by the Olympic Committee, but would only be on the U.C.I. list after the Tour.

Thus, the problems encountered during the 1998 Tour's "Festina Affair" and later the "TVM Affair" should come as no surprise. And once again it shows that the temptation of drug use is not limited to marginal riders but affects every tier of the peloton.

"The problem is that we expect athletes to be different from the rest of society," explains Cyrille Guimard, a long-time veteran of the sport. For over twenty years Guimard was a leading member of cycling's inner circle, first as a rider, then as the coach of seven Tour winners. Guimard knows what he is talking about. Perhaps he has even tasted some of that strange fruit himself. Certainly he has seen plenty of it around. "In today's pill-popping society we have medication for every ache and pain. The average Joe couldn't fathom the kinds of aches and pains inflicted on a rider in the Tour de France. But suddenly, because it is in the sports arena, it is forbidden."

Guimard also knows about aches and pains. As a star sprinter in the early 1970s he limped through the final week of the 1972 Tour de France crippled with tendonitis. Finally in the last days, with the green points jersey on his shoulders, Guimard had to abandon.

More recently, after the 1998 Tour de France, Doctor Bruno de Lignières, endocrinologist at the Paris Necker Hospital, went on record with the French daily *Le Monde* as saying that certain drugs could even be good for the health of the elite athlete, since they offered protection from the devastating deficiencies caused by sport. "It's important to know that intense, prolonged physical efforts induce hormonal imbalances that are detrimental

to one's health. But professional athletes are constantly forced to push themselves to such limits."

De Lignières maintains that many professional sports doctors in good conscience give their clients—in this case the athletes—the necessary drugs to realign these imbalances. The problem, however, is that many of the drugs they prescribe are forbidden by sporting federations and thus go against the ethics of sport.

Certainly as cycling moves into the twenty-first century we couldn't be any further from a common consensus concerning the drug question. Some say less than 20 percent of professional cyclists dope. Some put that figure at close to 100 percent. Unfortunately, many riders who are opposed to the principle of doping feel pressured

to join in simply to remain competitive—to keep their jobs.

In a related study, Bob Goldman, president of the National Academy of Sports Medicine, has surveyed Olympic-level American athletes concerning their views toward drug taking since 1982. According to the study over 50 percent of 198 athletes surveyed in 1995 said they would take a banned substance that would enable them to win every competition for five years, then kill them. Again, what are the options for those athletes who are against drugs? Do they still have any choice?

Visibly, the various branches of the sport seem equally divided. While certain teams have adopted charters with strict measures against riders caught doping, many teams resist such rules. All is

SWISS RIDER LAURENT DUFAUX TRIES TO FOCUS ON THE PROLOGUE IN DUBLIN.

fair in love and sport, they seem to be saying. And while Tour de France organizers are working with the International Olympic Committee to define exactly what constitutes doping in modern sport, they continue to find friction in the many sporting federations around the world who have clearly divergent ideas as to which products should be accepted and which should be forbidden.

Certainly cycling is not alone in this dilemma, and the drug problem confronts every elite sport. After the 1998 World Cup, the Italian Soccer Federation found itself bogged down in a similar doping quagmire, while American baseball's top slugger openly admits to using substances banned by the Olympic Committee.

Some have demanded that all records be abolished at the end of the millennium and that sports start the twenty-first century with a clean slate. Others instead demand that drug testing should be abolished, and in the laissez-faire spirit, athletes should be allowed to practice their own version of free enterprise, with all its inherent mutations.

How does that saying go? "So far we've come. But still so far to go." If one thing is clear, however, it is that the third millennium has been handed a prepackaged problem from the twentieth century.

LONG-TIME TOUR DIRECTOR JACQUES GODDET PLACES FLOWERS ON THE GRAVE OF TOM SIMPSON ON THE SUMMIT OF MONT VENTOUX.

TOUR RESULTS FROM 1903 TO THE PRESENT

RIDERS TAKING OFF ON THE FIRST STAGE OF THE 1903 TOUR DE FRANCE IN VILLENEUVE SAINT GEORGES. TOP PRERACE FAVORITES LIKE MAURICE GARIN AND HIPPOLYTE AUCOUTURIER ARE IN THE FOREGROUND.

While the yellow jersey, introduced in 1919, is most famous, several other distinctive jerseys distinguish winners of various sub-categories in the race. The green points jersey generally designates the race's most consistent sprinter (points winner), while the red polka-dot jersey designates the race's most consistent climber, and the recently re-introduced white jersey distinguishes the best young rider under 25.

1903:

1. Maurice Garin (Fr/La Française)
   2,428 kilometers in 94h 33min

2. Lucien Pothier (Fr) 2h 49min 45sec behind

3. Fernand Augereau (Fr) 4h 29min 38sec behind

1904:

1. Henri Cornet (Fr)
   2,428 kilometers in 96h 5min 55sec

2. Jean-Baptiste Dortignacq (Fr) 2h 16min 14sec behind

3. Eugène Catteau (Fr) 8h 7min 20sec behind

1905:

1. Louis Trousselier (Fr/Peugeot) 35 points*

2. Hippolyte Aucouturier (Fr) 61 pts

3. Jean-Baptiste Dortignacq (Fr) 64 pts

*From 1905 to 1912 the Tour was contested by points, with the lowest number of points winning.

1906:

1. René Pottier (Fr/Peugeot) 31 points

2. Georges Passerieu (Fr) 45 pts

3. Louis Trousselier (Fr) 59 pts

1907:

1. Lucien Petit-Breton (Fr/Peugeot) 47 points

2. Gustave Garrigou (Fr) 66 pts

3. Émile Georget (Fr) 74 pts

1908:

1. Lucien Petit-Breton (Fr/Peugeot) 36 points

2. François Faber (Lux) 68 pts

3. Georges Passerieu (Fr) 75 pts

1909:

1. François Faber (Lux/Alcyon) 37 points

2. Gustave Garrigou (Fr) 57 pts

3. Jean Alavoine (Fr) 66 pts

1910:

1. Octave Lapize (Fr/Alcyon) 63 points

2. François Faber (Lux) 67 pts

3. Gustave Garrigou (Fr) 86 pts

1911:

1. Gustave Garrigou (Fr/Alcyon) 43 points

2. Paul Duboc (Fr) 63 pts

3. Émile Georget (Fr) 84 pts

1912:

1. Odile Defraye (Bel/Alcyon) 49 points

2. Eugène Christophe (Fr) 108 pts

3. Gustave Garrigou (Fr) 140 pts

1913:

1. Philippe Thys (Bel/Peugeot)
   5,387 kilometers in 197h 54min*

2. Gustave Garrigou (Fr) 8min 37sec behind

3. Marcel Buysse (Bel) 30min 55sec behind

*In 1913 the Tour definitively returned to an overall time format, where the rider with the lowest combined time is declared the winner.

1914:

1. Philippe Thys (Bel/Peugeot)
   5,380 kilometers in 200h 28min 48sec

2. Henri Pélissier (Fr) 1min 40sec behind

3. Jean Alavoine (Fr) 36min 53sec behind

Due to World War I no Tour was held between 1915 and 1918.

1919:

1. Firmin Lambot (Bel/La Sportive)
   5,560 kilometers in 231h 7min 15sec

2. Jean Alavoine (Fr) 1h 32min 54sec behind

3. Eugène Christophe (Fr) 2h 16min 31sec behind

1920:

1. Philippe Thys (Bel/La Sportive)
   5,503 kilometers in 228h 36min 13sec

2. Hector Heusghem (Bel) 57min 21sec behind

3. Firmin Lambot (Bel) 1h 39min 35sec behind

1921:

1. Léon Scieur (Bel/La Sportive)
   5,485 kilometers in 221h 50min 26sec

2. Hector Heusghum (Bel) 18min 35sec behind

3. Honoré Barthélemy (Fr) 2h 1min behind

1922:

1. Firmin Lambot (Bel/Peugeot)
   5,375 kilometers in 222h 8min 6sec

2. Jean Alavoine (Fr) 41min 15sec behind

3. Félix Sellier (Bel) 43min 2sec behind

1923:
1. Henri Pélissier (Fr/Automoto)
   5,386 kilometers in 222h 15min 30sec

2. Ottavio Bottecchia (It) 30min 41sec behind

3. Romain Bellenger (Fr) 1h 4min 43sec behind

1924:
1. Ottavio Bottecchia (It/Automoto)
   5,425 kilometers in 226h 18min 21sec

2. Nicolas Frantz (Lux) 35min 36sec behind

3. Lucien Buysse (Bel) 1h 32min 13sec behind

1925:
1. Ottavio Bottecchia (It/Automoto)
   5,440 kilometers in 219h 10min 18sec

2. Lucien Buysse (Bel) 54min 20sec behind

3. Bartolomeo Aymo (It) 56min 17sec behind

1926:
1. Lucien Buysse (Bel/Automoto)
   5,745 kilometers in 238h 44min 25sec

2. Nicolas Frantz (Lux) 1h 22min 25sec behind

3. Bartolomeo Aymo (It) 1h 23min 51sec behind

1927:
1. Nicolas Frantz (Lux/Thomann)
   5,398 kilometers in 198h 16min 42sec

2. Maurice DeWaele (Bel) 1h 48min 21sec behind

3. Julien Veraecke (Bel) 2h 25min 6sec behind

1928:
1. Nicolas Frantz (Lux/Alcyon)
   5,476 kilometers in 192h 48min 58sec

2. André Leducq (Fr) 50min 7sec behind

3. Maurice DeWaele (Bel) 56min 16sec behind

1929:
1. Maurice DeWaele (Bel/Alcyon)
   5,286 kilometers in 186h 39min 16sec

2. Giuseppe Pancera (It) 44min 23sec behind

3. Jef Demuysère (Bel) 57min 10sec behind

1930:
1. André Leducq (Fr/French national team)
   4,822 kilometers in 172h 12min 16sec

2. Learco Guerra (It) 14min 13sec behind

3. Antonin Magne (Fr) 16min 3sec behind

1931:
1. Antonin Magne (Fr/French national team)
   5,091 kilometers in 177h 10min 3sec

2. Jef Demuysère (Bel) 12min 56sec behind

3. Antonio Pesenti (It) 22min 52sec behind

1932:
1. André Leducq (Fr/French national team)
   4,479 kilometers in 154h 12min 59sec

2. Kurt Stoepel (Ger) 24min 1sec behind

3. Francesco Camusso (It) 26min 11sec behind

1933:
1. Georges Speicher (Fr/French national team)
   4,395 kilometers in 147h 51min 37sec

2. Learco Guerra (It) 4min 1sec behind

3. Giuseppe Martano (It) 5min 8sec behind

Best Climber*: Vicente Trueba (Sp)

*Although the best-climber award began in 1933, it was not until 1975 that the leader of this category was distinguished with a polka-dot jersey.

1934:
1. Antonin Magne (Fr/French national team)
   4,470 kilometers in 147h 13min 58sec

2. Giuseppe Martano (It) 27min 31sec behind

3. Roger Lapébie (Fr) 52min 15sec behind

Best Climber: René Vietto (Fr)

1935:
1. Romain Maes (Bel/Belgian national team)
   4,338 kilometers in 141h 23min

2. Ambrosio Morelli (It) 17min 52sec behind

3. Félicien Vervaecke (Bel) 24min 6sec behind

Best Climber: Félicien Vervaecke (Bel)

1936:
1. Sylvère Maes (Bel/Belgian national team)
   4,442 kilometers in 142h 47min 32sec

2. Antonin Magne (Fr) 26min 55sec behind

3. Félicien Vervaecke (Bel) 27min 53sec behind

Best Climber: Julien Berrendero (Sp)

1937:
1. Roger Lapébie (Fr/French national team)
   4,415 kilometers in 138h 58min 31sec

2. Mario Vicini (It) 7min 17sec behind

3. Léo Amberg (Swz) 26min 23sec behind

Best Climber: Félicien Vervaecke (Bel)

1938:
1. Gino Bartali (It/Italian national team)
   4,694 kilometers in 148h 29min 12sec

2. Félicien Vervaecke (Bel) 18min 27sec behind

3. Victor Cosson (Fr) 29min 26sec behind

Best Climber: Gino Bartali (It)

1939:

1. Sylvère Maes (Bel/Belgian national team) 4,224 kilometers in 132h 3min 17sec

2. René Vietto (Fr) 30min 38sec behind

3. Lucien Vlaemynck (Bel) 32min 8sec behind

Best Climber: Sylvère Maes (Bel)

Due to World War II no Tour was held between 1940 and 1946.

1947:

1. Jean Robic (Fr/West French regional team) 4,640 kilometers in 148h 11min 25sec

2. Edouard Fachleitner (Fr) 3min 58sec behind

3. Pierre Brambilla (It) 10min 7sec behind

Best Climber: Pierre Brambilla (It)

1948:

1. Gino Bartali (It/Italian national team) 4,922 kilometers in 147h 10min 36sec

2. Albéric Schotte (Bel) 26min 16sec behind

3. Guy Lapébie (Fr) 28min 48sec behind

Best Climber: Gino Bartali (It)

1949:

1. Fausto Coppi (It/Italian national team) 4,808 kilometers in 149h 40min 49sec

2. Gino Bartali (It) 10min 55sec behind

3. Jacques Marinelli (Fr) 25min 13sec behind

Best Climber: Fausto Coppi (It)

1950:

1. Ferdi Kubler (Swz/Swiss national team) 4,775 kilometers in 145h 36min 46sec

2. Stan Ockers (Bel) 9min 30sec behind

3. Louison Bobet (Fr) 22min 19sec behind

Best Climber: Louison Bobet (Fr)

1951:

1. Hugo Koblet (Swz/Swiss national team) 4,690 kilometers in 142h 20min 14sec

2. Raphaël Geminiani (Fr) 22min behind

3. Lucien Lazaridès (Fr) 24min 16sec behind

Best Climber: Raphaël Geminiani (Fr)

1952:

1. Fausto Coppi (It/Italian national team) 4,898 kilometers in 151h 57min 20sec

2. Stan Ockers (Bel) 28min 27sec behind

3. Bernardo Ruiz (Sp) 34min 38sec behind

Best Climber: Fausto Coppi (It)

1953:

1. Louison Bobet (Fr/French national team) 4,476 kilometers in 129h 23min 25sec

2. Jean Malléjac (Fr) 14min 18sec behind

3. Giancarlo Astrua (It) 15min 1sec behind

Best Climber: Jésus Lorono (Sp)

Points Winner*: Fritz Schaer (Swz)

*Although a points competition was held in 1948 and 1949, it was not until 1953 that it became a permanent fixture in the Tour. The leader of this category wears a green jersey.

1954:

1. Louison Bobet (Fr/French national team) 4,656 kilometers in 140h 6min 5sec

2. Ferdi Kubler (Swz) 15min 49sec behind

3. Fritz Schaer (Swz) 21min 46sec behind

Best Climber: Federico Bahamontès (Sp)

Points Winner: Ferdi Kubler (Swz)

1955:

1. Louison Bobet (Fr/French national team) 4,495 kilometers in 130 h 29min 26sec

2. Jean Brankart (Bel) 4min 53sec behind

3. Charly Gaul (Lux) 11min 30sec behind

Best Climber: Charly Gaul (Lux)

Points Winner: Stan Ockers (Bel)

1956:

1. Roger Walkowiak (Fr/North-East Central regional team) 4,498 kilometers in 124h 1min 16sec

2. Gilbert Bauvin (Fr) 1min 25sec behind

3. Jean Adriaenssens (Bel) 3min 44sec behind

Best Climber: Charly Gaul (Lux)

Points Winner: Stan Ockers (Bel)

1957:

1. Jacques Anquetil (Fr/French national team) 4,686 kilometers in 135h 44min 42sec

2. Marcel Janssens (Bel) 14h 56min behind

3. Adolf Christian (Swz) 17min 20sec behind

Best Climber: Gastone Nencini (It)

Points Winner: Jean Forestier (Fr)

1958:

1. Charly Gaul (Lux/Dutch-Luxembourg mixed national team) 4,319 kilometers in 116h 59min 5sec

2. Vito Favero (It) 3min 10sec behind

3. Raphaël Geminiani (Fr) 3min 41sec behind

Best Climber: Federico Bahamontès (Sp)

Points Winner: Jean Graczyck (Fr)

1959:

1. Federico Bahamontès (Sp/Spanish national team) 4,391 kilometers in 123h 46min 45sec

2. Henri Anglade (Fr) 4min 1sec behind

3. Jacques Anquetil (Fr) 5min 5sec behind

Best Climber: Federico Bahamontès (Sp)

Points Winner: André Darrigade (Fr)

1960:

1. Gastone Nencini (It/Italian national team) 4,173 kilometers in 112h 8min 42sec

2. Graziano Battistini (It) 5min 2sec behind

3. Jean Adriaenssens (Bel) 10min 24sec behind

Best Climber: Imerio Massignan (It)

Points Winner: Jean Graczyck (Fr)

1961:

1. Jacques Anquetil (Fr/French national team) 4,397 kilometers in 122h 1min 33sec

2. Guido Carlesi (It) 12min 14sec behind

3. Charly Gaul (Lux) 12min 16sec behind

Best Climber: Imerio Massignan (It)

Points Winner: André Darrigade (Fr)

1962:

1. Jacques Anquetil (Fr/ACBB-St. Raphaël) 4,274 kilometers in 114h 31min 45sec

2. Joseph Planckaert (Bel) 4min 59sec behind

3. Raymond Poulidor (Fr) 10min 24sec behind

Best Climber: Federico Bahamontès (Sp)

Points Winner: Rudi Altig (Ger)

1963:

1. Jacques Anquetil (Fr/St. Raphaël) 4,210 kilometers in 113h 30min 5sec

2. Federico Bahamontès (Sp) 3min 35sec behind

3. José Perez-Frances (Sp) 10min 14sec behind

Best Climber: Federico Bahamontès (Sp)

Points Winner: Rik Van Looy (Bel)

1964:

1. Jacques Anquetil (Fr/St. Raphaël) 4,504 kilometers in 127h 9min 44sec

2. Raymond Poulidor (Fr) 55sec behind

3. Federico Bahamontès (Sp) 4min 44sec behind

Best Climber: Federico Bahamontès (Sp)

Points Winner: Jan Janssen (Hol)

1965:

1. Felice Gimondi (It/Salvarani) 4,188 kilometers in 116h 42min 6sec

2. Raymond Poulidor (Fr) 2min 40sec behind

3. Gianni Motta (It) 9min 18sec behind

Best Climber: Julio Jimenez (Sp)

Points Winner: Jan Janssen (Hol)

1966:

1. Lucien Aimar (Fr/Ford) 4,329 kilometers in 117h 34min 21sec

2. Jan Janssen (Hol) 1min 7sec behind

3. Raymond Poulidor (Fr) 2min 2sec behind

Best Climber: Julio Jimenez (Sp)

Points Winner: Willy Planckaert (Bel)

1967:

1. Roger Pingeon (Fr/French national team/Peugeot*) 4,780 kilometers in 136h 53min 50sec

2. Julio Jimenez (Sp) 3min 40sec behind

3. Franco Balmanion (It) 7min 23sec behind

*Please note that in 1967 and 1968 race organizers again experimented with national team structure. However, riders who rode with national team jerseys were also allowed to carry their commercial sponsors' logos.

Best Climber: Julio Jimenez (Sp)

Points Winner: Jan Janssen (Hol)

1968:

1. Jan Janssen (Hol/Dutch national team) 4,492 kilometers in 133h 49min 32sec

2. Herman Van Springel (Bel) 38sec behind

3. Ferdinand Bracke (Bel) 3min 3sec behind

Best Climber: Aurelio Gonzales (Sp)

Points Winner: Franco Bitossi (It)

1969:
1. Eddy Merckx (Bel/Faema)
   4,117 kilometers in 116h 16min 2sec

2. Roger Pingeon (Fr) 17min 54sec behind

3. Raymond Poulidor (Fr) 22min 13sec behind

Best Climber: Eddy Merckx (Bel)

Points Winner: Eddy Merckx (Bel)

1970:
1. Eddy Merckx (Bel/Faemino)
   4,254 kilometers in 119h 31min 49sec

2. Joop Zoetemelk (Hol) 12min 41sec behind

3. Gosta Petterson (Swd) 15min 54sec behind

Best Climber: Eddy Merckx (Bel)

Points Winner: Walter Godefroot (Bel)

1971:
1. Eddy Merckx (Bel/Molteni)
   3,608 kilometers in 96h 45min 14sec

2. Joop Zoetemelk (Hol) 9min 51sec behind

3. Lucien Van Impe (Bel) 11min 6sec behind

Best Climber: Lucien Van Impe (Bel)

Points Winner: Eddy Merckx (Bel)

1972:
1. Eddy Merckx (Bel/Molteni)
   3,846 kilometers in 108h 17min 18sec

2. Felice Gimondi (It) 10min 41sec behind

3. Raymond Poulidor (Fr) 11min 34sec behind

Best Climber: Lucien Van Impe (Bel)

Points Winner: Eddy Merckx (Bel)

1973:
1. Luis Ocana (Sp/Bic)
   4,090 kilometers in 122h 25min 34sec

2. Bernard Thévenet (Fr) 14min 51sec behind

3. Manuel Fuente (Sp) 17min 51sec behind

Best Climber: Pedro Torres (Sp)

Points Winner: Herman Van Springel (Bel)

1974:
1. Eddy Merckx (Bel/Molteni)
   4,098 kilometers in 116h 16min 58sec

2. Raymond Poulidor (Fr) 8min 4sec behind

3. Vicente Lopez-Carril (Sp) 8min 9sec behind

Best Climber: Domingo Perurena (Sp)

Points Winner: Patrick Sercu (Bel)

1975:
1. Bernard Thévenet (Fr/Peugeot)
   4,000 kilometers in 114h 35min 31sec

2. Eddy Merckx (Bel) 2min 47sec behind

3. Lucien Van Impe (Bel) 5min 1sec behind

Best Climber: Lucien Van Impe (Bel)

Points Winner: Rik Van Linden (Bel)

Best Young Rider: Francesco Moser (It)

1976:
1. Lucien Van Impe (Bel/Gitane)
   4,017 kilometers in 116h 22min 23sec

2. Joop Zoetemelk (Hol) 4min 14sec behind

3. Raymond Poulidor (Fr) 12min 8sec behind

Best Climber: Giancarlo Bellini (It)

Points Winner: Freddy Maertens (Bel)

Best Young Rider: Enrique Martinez-Heredia (Sp)

1977:
1. Bernard Thévenet (Fr/Peugeot)
   4,096 kilometers in 115h 38min 30sec

2. Hennie Kuiper (Hol) 48sec behind

3. Lucien Van Impe (Bel) 3min 32sec behind

Best Climber: Lucien Van Impe (Bel)

Points Winner: Jacques Esclassan (Fr)

Best Young Rider: Dietrich Thurau (Ger)

1978:
1. Bernard Hinault (Fr/Renault)
   3,908 kilometers in 108h 18min

2. Joop Zoetemelk (Hol) 3min 56sec behind

3. Joaquim Agostinho (Por) 6min 54sec behind

Best Climber: Mariano Martinez (Fr)

Points Winner: Freddy Maertens (Bel)

Best Young Rider: Henk Lubberding (Hol)

1979:
1. Bernard Hinault (Fr/Renault)
   3,765 kilometers in 103h 6min 50sec

2. Joop Zoetemelk (Hol) 3min 7sec behind

3. Joaquim Agostinho (Por) 26min 53sec behind

Best Climber: Giovanni Battaglin (It)

Points Winner: Bernard Hinault (Fr)

Best Young Rider: Jean-René Bernadeau (Fr)

1980:
1. Joop Zoetemelk (Hol/Ti-Raleigh)
   3,842 kilometers in 109h 19min 14sec

2. Hennie Kuiper (Hol) 6min 55sec behind

3. Raymond Martin (Fr) 7min 56sec behind

Best Climber: Raymond Martin (Fr)

Points Winner: Rudy Pevenage (Bel)

Best Young Rider: Johan van der Velde (Hol)

1981:

1. Bernard Hinault (Fr/Renault)
   3,753 kilometers in 96h 19min 38sec

2. Lucien Van Impe (Bel) 14min 34sec behind

3. Robert Alban (Fr) 17min 4sec behind

Best Climber: Lucien Van Impe (Bel)

Points Winner: Freddy Maertens (Bel)

Best Young Rider: Peter Winnen (Hol)

1982:

1. Bernard Hinault (Fr/Renault)
   3,507 kilometers in 92h 8min 46sec

2. Joop Zoetemelk (Hol) 6min 21sec behind

3. Johan Van de Velde (Hol) 8min 59sec behind

Best Climber: Bernard Vallet (Fr)

Points Winner: Sean Kelly (Ire)

Best Young Rider: Phil Anderson (Aus)

1983:

1. Laurent Fignon (Fr/Renault)
   3,809 kilometers in 105h 7min 52sec

2. Angel Arroyo (Sp) 4min 4sec behind

3. Peter Winnen (Hol) 4min 9sec behind

Best Climber: Lucien Van Impe (Bel)

Points Winner: Sean Kelly (Ire)

Best Young Rider: Laurent Fignon (Fr)

1984:

1. Laurent Fignon (Fr/Renault)
   4,021 kilometers in 112h 3min 40sec

2. Bernard Hinault (Fr) 10min 32sec behind

3. Greg LeMond (USA) 11min 46sec behind

Best Climber: Robert Millar (Scot)

Points Winner: Frank Hoste (Bel)

Best Young Rider: Greg LeMond (USA)

1985:

1. Bernard Hinault (Fr/La Vie Claire)
   4,109 kilometers in 113h 24min 23sec

2. Greg LeMond (USA) 1min 42sec behind

3. Stephen Roche (Fr) 4min 29sec behind

Best Climber: Luis Herrara (Col)

Points Winner: Sean Kelly (Ire)

Best Young Rider: Fabio Parra (Col)

1986:

1. Greg LeMond (USA/La Vie Claire)
   4,094 kilometers in 110h 35min 19sec

2. Bernard Hinault (Fr) 3min 10sec behind

3. Urs Zimmermann (Swz) 10min 54sec behind

Best Climber: Bernard Hinault (Fr)

Points Winner: Eric Vanderaerden (Bel)

Best Young Rider: Andy Hampsten (USA)

1987:

1. Stephen Roche (Ire/Carrera)
   4,231 kilometers in 115h 27min 42sec

2. Pedro Delgado (Sp) 40sec behind

3. Jean-François Bernard (Fr) 2min 13sec behind

Best Climber: Luis Herrera (Col)

Points Winner: Jean-Paul Van Poppel (Hol)

Best Young Rider: Raul Alcala (Mex)

1988:

1. Pedro Delgado (Sp/Reynolds)
   3,286 kilometers in 84h 27min 53sec

2. Stephen Rooks (Hol) 7min 13sec behind

3. Fabio Parra (Col) 9min 58sec behind

Best Climber: Steven Rooks (Hol)

Points Winner: Eddy Planckaert (Bel)

Best Young Rider: Eric Breukink (Hol)

1989:

1. Greg LeMond (USA/ADR)
   3,285 kilometers in 87h 38min 35sec

2. Laurent Fignon (Fr) 8sec behind

3. Pedro Delgado (Sp) 3min 34 behind

Best Climber: Gert-Jan Theunisse (Hol)

Points Winner: Sean Kelly (Ire)

Best Young Rider: Fabrice Philippot (Fr)

1990:

1. Greg LeMond (USA/Z)
   3,504 kilometers in 90h 43min 20sec

2. Claudio Chiappucci (It) 2min 16sec behind

3. Erik Breukink (Hol) 2min 29sec behind

Best Climber: Thierry Claveyrolat (Fr)

Points Winner: Olaf Ludwig (E. Ger)

Best Young Rider: Gilles Delion (Fr)

1991:

1. Miguel Indurain (Sp/Banesto)
   3,914 kilometers in 101h 1min 20sec

2. Gianni Bugno (It) 3min 36sec behind

3. Claudio Chiappucci (It) 5min 56sec behind

Best Climber: Claudio Chiappucci (It)

Points Winner: Djamolidine Abdoujaparov (Uz)

Best Young Rider: Alvaro Mejia (Mex)

1992:

1. Miguel Indurain (Sp/Banesto)
   3,983 kilometers in 100h 49min 30sec

2. Claudio Chiappucci (It) 4min 35sec behind

3. Gianni Bugno (It) 10min 49sec behind

Best Climber: Claudio Chiappucci (It)

Points Winner: Laurent Jalabert (Fr)

Best Young Rider: Eddy Bouwmans (Bel)

1993:

1. Miguel Indurain (Sp/Banesto)
   3,714 kilometers in 95h 57min 9sec

2. Tony Rominger (Swz) 4min 59sec behind

3. Zenon Jaskula (Pol) 5min 48sec behind

Best Climber: Tony Rominger (Swz)

Points Winner: Djamolidine Abdoujaparov (UZ)

Best Young Rider: Antonio Martin (Sp)

1994:

1. Miguel Indurain (Sp/Banesto)
   3,978 kilometers in 103h 38min 38sec

2. Piotr Ugrumov (Lit) 5min 39sec behind

3. Marco Pantani (It) 7min 19sec behind

Best Climber: Richard Virenque (Fr)

Points Winner: Djamolidine Abdoujaparov (UZ)

Best Young Rider: Marco Pantani (It)

1995:

1. Miguel Indurain (Sp/Banesto)
   3,635 kilometers in 92h 44min 59sec

2. Alex Zülle (Swz) 4min 35sec behind

3. Bjarne Riis (Den) 6min 47sec behind

Best Climber: Richard Virenque (Fr)

Points Winner: Laurent Jalabert (Fr)

Best Young Rider: Marco Pantani (It)

1996:

1. Bjarne Riis (Den/Deutsch Telekom)
   3,765 kilometers in 95h 57min 16sec

2. Jan Ullrich (Ger) 1min 41sec behind

3. Richard Virenque (Fr) 4min 37sec behind

Best Climber: Richard Virenque (Fr)

Points Winner: Erik Zabel (Ger)

Best Young Rider: Jan Ullrich (Ger)

1997:

1. Jan Ullrich (Ger/Deutsch Telekom)
   3,950 kilometers in 100h 30min 35sec

2. Richard Virenque (Fr) 9min 9sec behind

3. Marco Pantani (It) 14min 3sec behind

Best Climber: Richard Virenque (Fr)

Points Winner: Erik Zabel (Ger)

Best Young Rider: Jan Ullrich (Ger)

1998:

1. Marco Pantani (It/Mercatone-Uno)
   3,712 kilometers in 92h 49min 46sec

2. Jan Ullrich (Ger) 3min 21sec behind

3. Bobby Julich (USA) 4min 8sec behind

Best Climber: Christophe Rinero (Fr)

Points Winner: Erik Zabel (Ger)

Best Young Rider: Jan Ullrich (Ger)

1999:

1. Lance Armstrong (USA/U.S. Postal Service)
   3,687 kilometers in 91h 32min 16sec

2. Alex Zülle (Switz) 7min 37sec behind

3. Fernando Escartin (Spain) 10min 26sec behind

Best Climber: Richard Virenque (Fr)

Points Winner: Erik Zabel (Ger)

Best Young Rider: Benoit Salamon (Fr)

2000:

1. Lance Armstrong (USA/U.S. Postal Service)
   3,662 kilometers in 92h 33min 8sec

2. Jan Ullrich (Ger) 6min 2sec behind

3. Joseba Beloki (Sp) 10min 26sec behind

Best Climber: Santiago Botero (Col)

Points Winner: Erik Zabel (Ger)

Best Young Rider: Francisco Mancebo (Sp)

2001:

1. Lance Armstrong (USA/U.S. Postal Service)
   3,458 kilometers in 86h 17min 28sec

2. Jan Ullrich (Ger) 6min 44sec behind

3. Joseba Beloki (Sp) 9min 5sec behind

Best Climber: Laurent Jalabert (Fr)

Points Winner: Erik Zabel (Ger)

Best Young Rider: Oscar Sevilla (Sp)

2002:

1. Lance Armstrong (USA/U.S. Postal Service)
   3,282 kilometers in 82h 5min 12sec

2. Joseba Beloki (Sp) 7min 17sec behind

3. Raimondas Rumsas (Lit) 8min 17sec behind

Best Climber: Laurent Jalabert (Fr)

Points Winner: Robbie McEwen (Aus)

Best Young Rider: Ivan Basso (It)

ACKNOWLEDGMENTS

A thank you is in store for many. First, I would like to thank several teachers who have guided and inspired my work from the beginning. Thank you to Julie Badiee, Jeff Wolin, and Paul Kohl. Your friendship, encouragement, and discipline have shown me what it means to be a professional.

A very sincere thanks also goes to Samuel Abt of the *International Herald Tribune*, who has provided nothing but support, not to mention plenty of laughs, since I started covering bicycle racing. The countless hours spent in cars chasing "a bunch of guys pedaling in their underwear" just wouldn't have been the same without your company. Thanks also goes to John Wilcockson and my many friends with *VeloNews* who have been behind me from the start. John accepted my first story and provided encouragement when I was just coming into my own.

I am greatly indebted to Philip Heying, who always encouraged my cycling pictures, and to Agathe Gaillard at the Agathe Gaillard Gallery in Paris for first exhibiting my pictures of bike racers. In a milieu where sports are not often considered a viable subject matter, her courage to take chances remains unsurpassed.

This book would not have been possible if it were not for the continued commitment of Christina Wilson and Michael Carabetta at Chronicle Books.

With them, this project has been nothing but fun.

To the Société du Tour de France I also owe a big thanks for your open doors over the years and also for your continued efforts to maintain the integrity of the Tour, keeping it a sport first for the people. The millions of spectators who flock to the roads each year offer a testament to your success.

Many thanks to Mark Reidy of *Mountain Bike* for his help on the technical evolution of the bicycle and to cycling historian Serge Laget for his guidance and archival assistance.

I cherish the camaraderie of my many colleagues, friends, and family along the road: Rob Arnold, founder of *RIDE* magazine, Lionel Chami of *Le Parisien*, Gilles Comte and Fred Mons of *Vélo* magazine, Benoit Hopquin of *Le Monde*, Chris and Kathy Gutowsky at Crossroads Communication, Roger Knoebber and Philippe Aronson of the Dull Men's Club, Rupert Guinness, Greg Shapleigh, Andrew Taber, John D'Agostino, Guy Lorraine, Phil Toop, Lisa Scott, John Abt, Olivier Haralambon, Craig Cook, Eric Serres, Patrick Pizzanelli, Bertrand Pecquerie, Laurent Munnich, not to mention the many journalists at *L'Équipe*.

And last, thank you to the thousands of cyclists who have signed their name to the event—to the winners and most assuredly to those who did not win. Without your efforts, openness, and general good-willed simplicity, this seductive sport might have long ago been wrapped up and prepackaged in some stadium somewhere.

SELECTED BIBLIOGRAPHY

NEWSPAPERS AND MAGAZINES

L'Équipe, Paris, France

International Herald Tribune, Paris, France

La Gazzetta dello Sport, Milan, Italy

Libération, Paris, France

Miroir du Cyclisme, Paris, France

Le Monde, Paris, France

Le Parisien, Paris, France

Vélo Magazine, Paris, France

VeloNews, Boulder, CO. USA

BOOKS

Abt, Samuel. *Breakaway: On the Road with the Tour de France.* New York: Random House, 1985.

———— *In High Gear: The World of Professional Bicycle Racing.* Mill Valley, CA: Bicycle Books, 1989.

———— *LeMond: The Incredible Comeback of an American Hero.* New York: Random House, 1990.

———— *A Season in Turmoil: Lance Armstrong Replaces Greg LeMond as U.S. Cycling's Superstar.* Boulder, CO: VeloNews, 1995.

———— *Pedaling for Glory: Victory and Drama in Professional Bicycle Racing.* Osceola, WI: Bicycle Books, 1997.

Abt, Samuel, and James Startt. *In Pursuit of the Yellow Jersey.* San Francisco, CA: Vanderplatz Publications, 1999.

Augendre, Jacques. *Fausto Coppi.* Paris, France: Calmann-Lévy, 1997.

Blondin, Antoine. *L'Ironie du Sport.* Paris, France: Editions François Bourin, 1988.

Brunel, Philippe. *Le Tour de France Intime.* Paris, France: Calmann-Lévy, 1997.

Chany, Pierre. *La Fabuleuse Histoire du Tour de France.* Paris, France: Editions de La Martinière, 1995.

———— *La Fabuleuse Histoire du Cyclisme.* Paris, France: Editions de La Martinière, 1995.

———— *La Légende du Tour de France.* Geneva, Switzerland: Editions Liber, 1997.

———— *La Légende du Cyclisme.* Geneva, Switzerland: Editions Liber, 1997.

Dazat, Olivier. *Seigneurs et Forçats du Vélo.* Paris, France: Calmann-Lévy, 1997.

Guinness, Rupert. *The Foreign Legion.* Huddersfield, England: Springfield Books Limited, 1993.

Laget, Serge. *La Saga du Tour de France.* Paris, France: Découvertes Gaillimard, 1990.

Milenkovitch, Michel. *50 Histoires du Tour de France.* Paris, France: Editions du Spot, 1997.

Tergeen, François. *Les Géants du Cyclisme.* Paris, France: Les Editions Mondiales, 1958.

Vanwalleghem, Rik. *Eddy Merckx: The Greatest Cyclist of the 20th Century.* Boulder, CO: VeloNews, 1995.

YEARLY ALBUMS

L'Album du Cyclisme, Pierre Chany. Paris, France: Scandéditions, Multiple Years.

L'Année du Cyclisme, Claude Droussent. Paris, France: Calmann-Lévy, Multiple Years.

Le Livre D'Or du Cyclisme, Jean-Luc Gatelier and Jean François Quinet. Paris, France: Editions Solar, Multiple Years.

Le Monde Fabuleuse du Cyclisme, Henri Montulet. Paris, France: Winning International, Multiple Years.

Le Panorama d'Un Siècle: Guide Officiel du Tour de France. Paris, France: Societé du Tour de France, Multiple Years.

Tour de France: Le Livre Officiel. Paris, France: Editions Solar, Multiple Years.

TOUR DE FRANCE/TOUR DE FORCE: PHOTO CREDITS

FRIENDS OF JACQUES-HENRI LARTIGUE ASSOCIATION:
46–47.

KEYSTONE PHOTO ARCHIVES:
Back Cover, 3, 6, 22, 39, 40, 42, 43 (right), 48, 49,
50, 51, 53 (all), 54, 57, 58, 59, 60, 61 (left), 63 (all),
64, 65, 66, 67 (all), 68, 69, 70, 71, 72, 73, 74, 75,
76, 78, 80, 81, 82, 85, 86, 89, 94, 95, 97, 143, 145.

FRED MONS:
100.

**COMPLIMENTS OF THE ORGANIZATIONAL COMMITTEE FOR THE
1999 WORLD CHAMPIONSHIPS:**
62.

PHOTOSPORT/MIROIR ARCHIVES:
5, 55, 61 (right), 79, 84, 87, 88, 89, 90, 91, 92, 93 (all),
101, 103, 104, 106, 107, 108, 140, 145, 147 (bottom).

SERGE LAGET COLLECTION:
1, 2, 16, 18, 19, 20, 23, 24, 25, 26, 27 (all), 28, 29,
30, 31, 32, 33, 34, 35, 36, 37 (all), 38, 43 (left),
52 (all), 53, 56, 148.

JAMES STARTT PHOTOS:
Front Cover, 4, 7, 8, 105, 109, 110, 112, 113, 114,
115 (all), 116, 117, 118, 119 (all), 121, 122, 123,
124, 125, 126, 127, 128-29, 130, 131, 132 (all),
133, 134, 135, 136, 137, 138 (all), 139 (all), 144,
146, 147 (upper), 159, 160.